...hit from behind. . .

Out of perfect timing came perfect chaos...

by
  Jim Heckel

PRESS

This book is dedicated to Jesus Christ.

Table of Contents

Life can change in a second. We all will be or have been hit from behind.

Psalm 46:

God is our refuge and strength,
an ever-present help in trouble.

Therefore we will not fear, though the earth give way
and the mountains fall into the heart of the sea,

though its waters roar and foam
and the mountains quake with their surging.
Selah

There is a river whose streams make glad the city of God,
the holy place where the Most High dwells.

God is within her, she will not fall;
God will help her at break of day.

Nations are in uproar, kingdoms fall;
he lifts his voice, the earth melts.

The Lord Almighty is with us;
the God of Jacob is our fortress.
Selah

Come and see the works of the Lord,
the desolations he has brought on the earth.

He makes wars cease to the ends of the earth;
he breaks the bow and shatters the spear,
he burns the shields with fire.

"Be still, and know that I am God;
I will be exalted among the nations,
I will be exalted in the earth."

The Lord Almighty is with us;
the God of Jacob is our fortress.
Selah

Preface

⸺᷍

This book is dedicated to Jesus Christ. Why? He fixed my life. If I were to dedicate this book to anyone else, it would have to be my wife, Beth. I've known her since age 15, and now I am approaching 60. We've been married for more than 33 years. She's seen the absolute worst side of me, yet stood by me. She's seen some of the (albeit small) good things that I've done and helped me to cultivate those minor good things. In essence, she's my eternal life-mate, so this book is also deeply dedicated to her.

In terms of dedication, close behind her are my children, Aimee and Nathan. They also saw and experienced some bad times due to my behaviors. The amazing thing is that they turned out, in my humble opinion, perfect. I attribute this mostly to my wife.

My editor was my daughter, Aimee Heckel, who has her under-graduate degrees from Colorado State University, both in journalism and German. She is presently a journalist in Colorado and has won several distinguished awards both from a local and national level. She was not only my editor, but also an active participant in the development of this book. She was my writing coach, my mentor and she gave me the passion to work on my writing skills. Mine may pale in comparison to hers, but knowing her eyes have helped with this project gives me a great sense of pride and relief.

In this book, I have laid my cards on the table, and I hope that you know that this author is on a journey that is aimed at getting better over time and not the converse. In fact, the older I get, the more I realize that, through God's grace, this is actually possible.

We can actually improve over time if we give our lives to God's care and feeding. Even when we get "hit from behind," we can grow. And that is the central premise of even attempting this being my first book. While I've written many papers in college, published articles and authored many other things, this is the first attempt to broaden my audience and publish a book. Thanks again, Aimee.

This book is not a huge dissertation or an expository type of work. Rather, it is a short story about an accident that happened to our family in the summer of 2007. This book is designed to be read in less than eight hours. We're already over-taxed by tons of email, text messages on our phones and the simple exposure to an infinite amount of information. I love to read, but huge novels are not my favorites. I call this an "airplane book," which means that you should be able to read this on a short flight, or if you need something to put you to sleep at night.

If you're on a plane reading this, then I hope that it's an easy read and one that you can do instead of working on some spreadsheet for work. If you're reading this in the quiet solitude of your home, put on a pot of coffee and relax. If you're reading this on your lunch hour, spread it over a few days and before you know it, you'll be finished.

Maybe there's just one sentence in this short book that jumps out to you that helps you in your Christian walk. Or if you are not a Christian, then maybe you will be able to get a glimpse of something into what this whole Christian thing is about that may be missing in your life.

So please read this book with an open mind. Read this book with an open heart. I thank you for allowing me to share. Perhaps by doing so, through my poor attempt to capture the unexplainable on paper, you may gain some insight into your own spiritual journey, whatever that may be and whoever you might worship. We all worship someone or something, it is human nature and is hardly deniable.

Chapter 1

The Steely Taste and the Purpose of This Book

—⟳—

The steely taste of something behind my clogged nose and in the back of my throat, coupled with pounding throbbing of my heart, gives me a sense of panic, being out of control, and my destiny untouchable by my own efforts.

If you've ever been hit really hard in a car accident or by a fist, or taken a nasty hit of any kind to the head or chest, you know this feeling. It's worse than simply having the wind knocked out of you. It has a distinctly scary taste in the back part of your tongue.

You can taste it in your throat and even on the roof of your mouth. It's like the taste of a penny in your mouth, but it permeates throughout your head into your sinuses and clouds your mind in a scary way. Maybe it's the taste of shock? Maybe it's the taste of blood?

Not that I can vividly remember anything, only partial slivers of opaquely gray and black consciousness that came and went, somewhat randomly, and very disturbingly.

Imagine hauling a large, heavy mirror into your back yard on a hot summer day. You're standing right in the sun. It's sweltering hot, and when you carry the mirror, you can see yourself in the reflection, arms struggling with the weight of the mirror, and the intense, bright sunshine piercing into your eyes. You prop the mirror against a lawn chair. Then, you take a brick and hurl it at the mirror at full force. Glass shards go flying all over the place and the once nice mirror is now in pieces, some large, some small but all were once connected in a very organized way. Now the mirror is a dangerous mess of sharp glass embedded in your lawn.

My job is to clean up this mess by trying to pick up all of the pieces littered in the blades of grass and glue them back together. It will never be the same so if I get most of it cleaned up and re-assembled, the mirror can still have some utility.

And did I mention that I have no sunglasses?

Those splintered but sharply reflective shards of memory do not make any coherent picture of what happened on this August after-noon in 2007, so trying to put this broken mess together may never make sense, and it's a dangerous undertaking. I know I'll never fuse it all back together because some of the pieces are now deeply embedded in the grass and will never be retrieved. I'm only going for the large pieces and acknowledge that it's tedious work that will always have scars and incompleteness. Some of the glass shards cut me when I sift through the grass. But I feel that I need to complete picking up the mess and cleaning it up the best that I can.

That's my warning and also my excuse for trying to document this experience, when in actuality, I'm probably the least qualified to do so.

This book you hold in your hands is not about me, it's about you.

Who are you? What relationship do you have with God? Do you even believe there is a God? Why do bad things happen? Where will you spend eternity? People come into our lives to teach us more about ourselves. So my experience is your experience. So are my lessons. So is my awakening.

This is about an awakening in my life during the past few years where I've had to redefine Christianity, not as a religion, but in terms of a relationship with Jesus Christ. There is a huge difference. I hope that this book will first give God all His due glory, and secondly, help you when — not if — you get "hit from behind." It will happen, maybe not literally like it was with me when I was struck by a car whilst riding my bike, but figuratively you will go through some tough times.

Life is full of surprises, some good, some not so good, espe-cially if you're trying to live for Him. The important thing is how we handle those not-so-good experiences. And please note that from the outset, if you could rate Christians on a scale of one to 10 (where 10 is next to being like God), I'd probably be lucky to get a two.

So why read a book about this timeless question – why does God let bad things happen? — written by such a novice, in terms of the Christian life? After all, if you wanted to get better at your golf game, you wouldn't read a book by an author who has a golf handicap of 30 (which, incidentally is mine). Instead, you'd prob-ably choose to read a book by a pro golfer. If you wanted to learn how to pass your CPA examination, you wouldn't read a book by a person that knows little about accounting.

But Christianity is unlike a hobby or a profession. It's about living with a purpose, living with security and living a life of learning. Christianity is not an activity you add on top of your life, it is the foundation below your life. If you were to watch a video of my life, you would see huge mistakes. You would see inconsistencies that make you sick. You would see a person that has made (almost) every mistake known to man. Running down the list of the 10 command-ments, I fall guilty of them all, literally or figuratively as The Bible explains them.

The other thing that you would see is God's amazing patience and His ability to forgive. You would see His unending love. You'd see the grace that He offered to a pretty nasty person: me.

So carrying this logic one step further, I can honestly say that based on my many mistakes, I could be an authority on mistakes. These are my credentials. And so, by reading this book, perhaps you can learn from my mistakes and lessons. While being innocently hit on a bike ride clearly was not my mistake, it certainly has made me contemplate many of the area in my own life where mistakes were, in fact, made.

But before we go there, here is the roadmap of where we're going: the purpose of this book.

The Purpose of This Book

On Aug. 3, 2007, while riding my bike, I was hit from behind by a car, almost costing me my life. One moment things were fine. The next, life changed dramatically for my family, friends and some people who I didn't even know.

In this book, I wish to share this experience, some of my lessons and feelings, and somehow I hope to bring glory to God Almighty.

The main purpose of this book is twofold:

1) **To give honor and glory to Jesus Christ**, taking what some may call a "very bad experience," and to turn it into a positive experience, and;

2) **To help our brothers and sisters in Africa** who are now (as you read this) dying from unhealthy living conditions (such as malaria, AIDS and other related kinds of preventable diseases). Over 75% of proceeds of this book will go to support Think Humanity (www.thinkhumanity.org), which is my family's nonprofit organization designed to prevent malaria and care for refugees and orphans in Uganda, just one more example of how a tragedy can bring good, stirring ripples you might never foresee. I'll explain more about Think Humanity later.

To give honor and glory to Jesus Christ

During and after the accident, I was confined to a bed and a wheel chair. I had plenty of quiet, down-time to talk with God and wonder why this happened to me. Sometimes, I actually felt mad at my Lord, in a way. How could a loving God let such a terrible thing happen to someone who has accepted Him as their personal Savior? Finally after trying my best to figure out this whole Christian gig, why did God allow this to occur?

These are just some of the many questions that rambled through my mind during times in the hospital, lying alone at night on a rented hospital bed in the downstairs of my home, and even months later while driving my truck and approaching a biker in the bike lane.

I would become amazed when I started to list the many things that I learned as a result of the experience. The number one thing that I learned was that God never puts us through more than what we can handle through His grace. If somehow, maybe one reader who is now suffering from some physical, emotional or spiritual hurt can glean a closer relationship with Christ from my experience, then the main objective of this book has been fulfilled.

To help fund our brothers and sisters in Africa dying from unhealthy living conditions in Africa

Two years before the accident, my daughter, Aimee, a journalist, made a trip to Africa to write about a Colorado nonprofit, Educate! organization, which provides scholarships and leadership training for refugees and orphans on the Kyangwali Refugee Camp in western Uganda. Aimee wrote an award-winning article about the efforts of this organization.

At the same time, our church launched a program that focused on Christ, compassion and community. Looking back, these were not random events. In fact, these events lined up to inspire my wife to begin selling books on eBay to raise money for Educate!.

Further accentuating this has been the singer Bono's challenge to the Body of Christ (denomination intentionally omitted!) to help those in need, underscoring the seemingly blatant (in most cases) disregard for the injustice of people dying as a result of where they've been born.

Then about a year later, my wife started selling books on eBay to fund educational opportunities (through the Educate organization, www.educateafrica.org) for people in Kyangwali. She worked tirelessly collecting books at secondhand bookstores to resell on eBay to raise money for the orphans and refugees.

While in this process, she also became "upset" (burdened) about the many people who were dying as a result of malaria in the same refugee settlement of roughly 20,000 people. That led us to form a nonprofit organization called Think Humanity, to ship malaria medication and mosquito nets to the refugees in need.

This eventually landed my daughter and wife to plan a humanitarian trip to Africa in mid-August 2007. Scheduled the same week as my accident.

This trip would help affect more than just the refugees, but we didn't know that when we planned it.

Think Humanity will take its efforts as far as God continues to lead us, while we listen to Him and obey Him. If by selling a few copies of this book, we can follow God's commandment to help the poor (referenced more than 2,000 times in the Bible), then this second objective has been met.

I must confess: There is a third purpose of this book, too.

Maybe I'm writing out of excitement, happiness and joy that I craved years ago and couldn't find. Maybe it lies in the peace that I really do have at this juncture in life. Maybe it's witnessing how true Christianity really should work (e.g. my daughter's recent gift of servitude for victims of the Katrina Hurricane). Maybe it's appreciation for a wife, who didn't give up on me, despite my deep-rooted sin issues. Maybe it's how my son tells me about something he's recently learned from attending a worship service in Dallas. Maybe it's the fact that I recovered to about 75% and am thankful to simply to be alive.

I guess it's all of those things.

I also know I am inspired by finally appreciating the patience God has had putting up with my nonsense for most of my life, and not giving up on me. But the reason really doesn't matter. What does matter now for me is to make up some lost time, and spend the balance of my time on this planet to do His will and bank a bit on my Eternal Retirement Plan.

Chapter 2

Back Pedaling a Few Years and Christianity Redefined

—◌〉

I'm pretty much a normal average guy. Five-six, 150 pounds, shaved bald head. I married my high-school sweetheart some 35 years ago (I bumping 60) and became a Christian as a young man. I received my MBA from the University of Wyoming in 1976 and began my career in the corporate world, where I have worked for more than 30 years, upon graduating from The University of Wyoming. My nickname is Frog, for some reason. Maybe it's because I look like one or like bugs, given I'm an avid fly fisher. Anyway, that's my name.

I never made it very high in the corporate world, but did OK, peaking out at second-level management. I worked in a lot of different areas within the corporation management realms from Manufacturing to Procurement and now in IT. It seems like I changed jobs about every few years, which always kept me learning new things. Pretty much I've traveled around the world, which is one of the perks of being in the corporate scene. And of recent I somehow survived the massive lay-offs in the wake of the September 11 terrorist attacks.

My wife and I grew up in northern Illinois and moved to Colorado a couple of years after our marriage. We lived in Chicago for a few years as well. Colorado has a special place in our hearts, because we love the mountains, and I'm an avid outdoors guy, from mountain-biking to simply working in the yard.

Getting my undergraduate degree from the University of Illinois at Chicago Circle Campus and living in the inner city of Chicago, we had some rough experiences (someone tried to rape my wife) and decided that it was time to move. Two days after that incident, we were in Arvada, Colorado with all of our earthly possessions totaling around $1,000 (including our 1971 Pinto).

We now have two wonderful children, a daughter and a son. They both live nearby and our family is very close. We've had our share of good times, as well as the bad times. We've traveled across the globe together, watched my son win soccer matches and laughed together when my daughter caught her pom-pons on fire cheering a football game. Behind the white picket fence (yes, we literally have one of those in our front yard), we've also stuck together through deaths of pets, my wife's genetic and rare brain disease, my daughter's admitted bad taste in boyfriends and my own battles with alcoholism.

We weren't always "church-goers" until a few years back when my drinking almost destroyed our family altogether.

After moving to Colorado, my wife and I gave up the church scene. I hated organized religion and rejected it for more than two decades. The hypocrisy and man-made rules drove me nuts. I felt that God gave me a mind of my own.

I would eventually have to 'redefine' Christianity for myself. And it would come from first having a re-born need for such, coupled with a provisionary solution.

The need came from the alcohol, a potentially cataclysmic issue in my life that was draining my very existence and that of my family's. Never mind the details, but suffice it to say that I had a series of problems that were becoming worse over time. From hiding a drinking problem, an extra-marital affair, lying, cheating, being dishonest, just points to a few of the 10 commandments that I've demolished.

I am relieved to know that the festering of these problems only escalated to a rather voluminous noise level, but never reached ear-deafening decibels. Somehow people put up with me. I now know the meaning of love.

My son and daughter tried numerous times to get me to stop drinking, but there was always some excuse continuing. Job pressures. The stress of having to mow the lawn. The stress of having to watch TV, even the stress to stop drinking. Any excuse. A person with a drinking problem will always find a reason to drink. Always. I tried only drinking on weekends. That meant that I was torched from Friday afternoon till Sunday night. I tried to limit my intake of booze by only buying it on certain days. That failed. So I gave up trying to quit drinking and never thought about asking God to help me. At the peak of my boozing, I figured I was consuming over 10,000 calories per week of alcohol related products. I also was a runner and figured that for every mile I ran, that equated to around one light beer. So the more I ran, the more I could drink. Running with a hang-over is very nasty for the first few miles!

The provisionary solution was discovered in a church in our local town.

One summer afternoon, my son invited me to attend this church. Having slugged down a couple of beers mowing the lawn in my shorts and tank top, I thought, "What the hell, I'll go."

But this church was different. It served Starbucks coffee (which helped sober me up), played loud Christian rock music and no one cared about what you wore or how you looked. I liked it. We started going to church.

This church turned religion into a "relationship" with Christ, never minding some of the legalistic, man-made items (items that relate to one's convictions), that seem to demean Christianity. This Church helped me to realize that my relationship with Christ was most important, and then the details follow as a result of the Holy Spirit working in one's life. Isn't this what Paul talks about in the book to the Romans? Once I began to 'redefine' Christianity in my own mind, and with God's patience, I got my life squared away.

God's patience is amazing, and His grace beyond my human comprehension. Thanks to God's help, my son and I have been sober for more than three years. One night I was drunk (again) and my son took me out into 'the garage.' The garage is the men's place to talk, chew tobacco, spit and bond. He told me to my face, "Frog, if you don't stop drinking, then I'm not going to hang around anymore." WOW! Talk about a wake-up call from your son. This was my fishing buddy! My daughter had also said the same on many occasions and, of course, I promised to slow down my drinking and I did for a small time. My wife also was hurt many times as a result of my drinking. And concurrently, my son was developing the exact same drinking problem (funny how that works). So around mid summer 2005, we both made a pact to stop drinking. And we've kept that pack, thanks to the Power of God. The funny part is that to this day, I don't believe that alcohol is a sin, in and of itself, but the way I had been abusing it most certainly was. Drinking alcohol is a convictional matter with the individual. It's like anything that becomes between you and God, from playing too much golf, fishing instead of working, buying excessive amounts of toys and not being able to pay your light bill, to (in my case) getting drunk every night.

I wish I could say that ever since that day of coming back to God our family had no more problems, but that would be a lie. In fact, we may have more problems now than we used to have. The point simply stated, we still have plenty of problems.

But there are two key points about these problems:
1. They aren't the same type of problems, like (for me) getting drunk every night.
2. We handle our problems differently than we used to. We give them to God to solve. Make no mistake, we don't have it all figured out. I'm not preaching about a how to be a good Christian. Rather, I'm talking about how God's patience has spared a proud and screwed up man.

Without all of this – my family, our proven ability to fight through the tough times, my new church family and strong relationship with God and this new way of dealing with problems — I couldn't have survived that terrible August day, which brings me to the point of my 'redefinition' of Christianity.

Christianity or Insanity?

While reflecting back on how my personal issues regressed over time, some of it stemmed from an arcane and debilitating definition of Christianity. I call this, close but distant, Insanity. Insanity, within the context of Christianity, involves the kind of foundational primary focus on legalistic tenets that was promulgated during my childhood while attending a fundamental church.

Such tenets (any of a set of established and fundamental beliefs, especially one relating to religion or politics) took the Biblical truths and marred them to accommodate specific and very narrow interpretation by a given human being, in this case, the pastor. Such tenets actually focused on issues where the Bible is not vividly clear and, thus, sought out clarification and definition under the auspices of some higher level of Biblical knowledge or authority.

A ridiculous, but real, example would be the act of women wearing jeans. In this example, the Bible only states that women are to dress modestly so as not to be an enabler of "lust of the flesh." Maybe there is a scripture verse that directly confronts the act of women wearing long clothing over their legs, but as of today, I haven't found such. Continuing with this example in my childhood church, our pastor decreed from the pulpit that, due to the superiority of his Biblical interpretation over ours, women would commit sin by the mere act of wearing of jeans. While this example may sound extreme, it pales by comparison to other tenets and legalistic dictums offered within the context their favorite, and most quoted, verse, "...be ye separate."

Such tenets served as a fine foundation for their so-called doctrinal non-acceptance of people who interpreted the unclear Biblical teachings different than the pastor did. Hey, don't argue with the pastor!

The cycle continues to support itself with the "separation" verse. The more one is separate, the better. The more discriminate, the better. The less you do "of the world," the better. The more that one (presumably the pastor) can "invent" separation, the better (obviously). And so goes the cycle. This cycle grows to amazingly large proportions until it virtually drains most of the joyful elements of what I now term Christianity, until it virtually strips Christianity of the personal relationship with Jesus. It becomes about rules, with little space for grace. And guilt is centerpiece. If you left the church feeling like a sack of crap, then the pastor succeeded. If you left with a smile on your face, then you obviously didn't 'get it.'

The results?

This is not only dangerous for individuals, who feel pushed away from Christianity, but also for the overall scene.

One day a few years back, I sat in on a church that practiced this so-called insanity. Here's what I saw:

- **Lack of growth.** This church has about 300 members and has not grown appreciably in 25 years. Members have built onto their building, but the church is far from at its physical capacity. People seem to go to church out of guilt, not out of desire.
- **A dead "flavor" of Christianity.** Joy is not obvious to a casual visitor. People are pretty much in a hole, peeking out now and then. (I use the term "hole" versus "rut" as the rut at least has some direction). Happiness is replaced with guilt. The focus is always on the negative. The music resembles what one would expect to hear in Purgatory. Routine substitutes for spontaneity and nary a laugh, despite the poor jokes that are preplanned, rehearsed and carefully written down in the predictable three-point message outline. Most people sleep. There is no youth ministry.

  You do the math. The life and visceral energy from each person is sapped upon walking through the front door. Just ask my wife. She had to purchase a pair of high-top boots to cover up her ankle tattoos (wrong according to some religions) before even feeling like she could enter the church. (Come to think of it, maybe women aren't supposed to wear boots...)
- **People view this type of worship as something that affords little.** When I asked my friend if he wanted to go

with us to church, he was quick to point out that he doesn't go to church, even though he is claims to be a Christian. His son refuses to go and would rather watch WWF on the tube. Other visitors who attend leave and seldom return. The church of Insanity is not relevant to our world today; therefore, people cannot identify or make any rational sense out of it. It's its own little comatose cosmos that inches through time, barely breaking even in the process. It takes no imagination to know that this church almost has to beg people to attend. There's little relevance for anyone in today's world.

- **People are more concerned with how you are conforming to their legal tenets than the true meaning of Christianity.** I base this on the content and theme of the message we heard. It was about Lot and how he went to Sodom and sold his daughters as harlots. The central theme was how, when associated with the world (Sodom), one becomes like the world, and then one goes down the tubes big time. Of course "be ye separate" was a cornerstone of the message. I'm not denying the fact that Christians are 'separate,' yet we are expected to live in our world that God made. Here, I feel the word 'separate' is more akin to an 'arrogant segregation,' or piety.

At the end of each message an alter call is given to the congregation and people are asked to make life-changing commitments, guilt-driven. At this message, the commitment wasn't about a life-changing commitment to follow Christ. It was about a life-changing commitment to not be "worldly," where worldly is again defined by the pastor's tenets on issues where the Bible is vague (dress, association, activities, convictions, methods of evangelism, physical appearance, spending, Bible translations – (King James Version only spoken here).

The blind follow the blind. People have checked out. They have turned off their brains and follow what is said from the pulpit. This sort of radical fundamentalism helps me understand why some Americans are concerned about radical Islam. While I don't fear for my life when I attended this church, the covert disdain for "outsiders" clearly is felt.

25

Perhaps they have their own little Jihad in mind when they sing "Onward Christian Soldiers?" (We'll return to the military metaphor in a bit.)

This religion grows contrary to both our God-given intellect and the verse that states " For there is one God and one mediator between God and men, the man Christ Jesus" (1 Tim2:5). If there is only one mediator, the Man Christ Jesus and if I accept Him as my personal Savior, then shouldn't He also convict me and teach me, through God's Word, what behaviors I can and cannot do? Why do I need a preacher to tell me I can or cannot perform various behaviors? Are they more "God literate" than I?

Doctrinal teachings notwithstanding, <u>such tenets can destroy an otherwise "good" church</u>. The love of Christ — the closeness of a personal relationship with God — is only spoken about and not lived by the congregation, who follow the pastor into realms resembling, and very easily imaginable, Kool-Aid drinking by Jim Jones some time ago. The negative cycle and spiral of separation feeds on itself until a cog in this vicious gear breaks or until someone starts thinking.

Being a young man and wanting to discover life, I mistakenly ventured deeper into such legalistic Insanity by attending a non-denominational fundamental college. It was at this college that I began my rebellion from this Insanity concept. I started to think for myself and took it to the ultimate extreme. This extreme living essentially ignored God altogether. I sought my selfishness, my own personal interests and conducted my life as I 'damned well pleased.'

Such rebellion continued throughout my life and festered to the point of swinging 180 degrees, to the opposite end of either Christianity or Insanity. This was kind of like rejecting almost both extremes. While my personal faith in Christ <u>as my only hope</u> failed to change, my regressive growth as a Christian (defined as a relationship with Christ) most certainly did.

Ultimately, such regression will either result in some cataclysmic event (divorce, prison, arrests, loss of something valuable or even death) or continue its cancerous eating away at core values until spiritual death occurs. Surfing between the waves seems to go nowhere but down. Through the medium of relevant music, something that's always been rebelliously important to me, coupled with a 'redefinition' of Christianity is where I find myself now.

In this rediscovery process, my wife and I found that God's word is not so complex, and it affords all of the same amazing power. This new definition stems from a few key, but critical, elements:

1. **The focus on the true joy of a personal relationship with God**. While the Insanity version says these words, they only scratch the surface. This is where Christianity all begins and ends. This key and critical concept means that you are an intelligent being and that God can speak to you alone, with no need for formal interpretation by people purported to be more "God literate." Convictions (not tenets) will be directed by God and interpreted individually by each through the Holy Spirit. For example, some people can drink alcohol with no problems. The Bible is not crystal clear on alcohol usage and yet in Insanity, "prohibition" is a key tenet. Beyond this example, *whatever* keeps you from being closer to God and inserts sin into one's life is simply to be either eliminated or avoided. In studying the Old Testament, one could boil down idolatry into the definition of anything that keeps you from developing a closer relationship with God. Anything. Even following blind "Christian" tenets.

2. **The personal respect for Biblical interpretation (ties into No. 1) and full acceptance of the multiplicity of worship styles.** *This* is the Body of Christ (aka the church in its largest context). Analogous would be an army of soldiers sent to battle. *Their unification is paramount to winning the battle* and leaves no room for segregation based upon which type of rifle is preferred for a given battle. The commander needs to be on the front line thereby demonstrating her or his equality with others and commitment. Continuing this metaphor, a commander who stands behind the troops and simply critiques their weaponry is not a commander, but rather a coward. Furthermore, such commanders who wield their own weapons upon their own soldiers, based upon difference in how they fight, are doing more for the enemy than their

objective! Having a liberal acceptance for Christians of a different worship/conviction style yields no death in friendly fire and gives a much truer sense of the love of Christ.

When the 12 disciples set out to change the world, it's highly unlikely that they first focused on tenets or differences, versus focusing on the commonality of the doctrine of salvation through Jesus. Of course, now the challenge for *me* is to somehow accept (even) the Insane versions of Christianity!

3. **The relevance of an Old Gospel for today's world and the allowance and freedom of expression.** The Great Commission in Mark 16:15,16 states, "Go into all the world and preach the good news to all creation. Whoever believes and is baptized will be saved, but whoever does not believe will be condemned." This commandment seems more possible today than ever, given the advent of our technological tools for information dissemination. Why should other aspects of our current culture (music, dress, appearance, certain activities one chooses, etc.) be any different? According to John, the "world" comprises of only three things: "the lust of the eye, the lust of the flesh and the pride of heart." Separating ourselves from the "world" (being "worldly") means to focus on these elements, not whether roller-skating to rock music resembles dancing, which resembles sex, which is bad. Tenets are man-made, not necessarily God-commanded.

4. **Our highest and ultimate calling is to do God's will.** Our purpose is to demonstrate the love of God through our actions, thereby exemplifying an aspired-to life. While Christ was on the planet, people came to know Him by his exemplary life, not by Him deciding on whether or not women should wear jeans. If our everyday life is centered on being close to Him, our "fruits will bear." This is supported in Mat 7:20, "Thus, by their fruit you will recognize them." This applies to road rage, cutting in line at the grocery store, reading the Bible, talking to God all of the time, how we approach our work and accepting (even) those who disagree with my definition of Christianity. Why aren't people jumping at the chance to

become a Christian? Pretty much, our fruits don't demonstrate God's Love.

Digging deeper into the definition emerges an irony with my 'new definition.' I am being guilty (here comes the guilt gene!) of the same things that upset my course some years ago. I acknowledge that the word "insanity" is a bit tough on people who choose that tight and tenet-filled pathway. These people are on our side. They are in our army of soldiers.

The central difference, however, is the method by which I will approach this cognitive dissonance. Instead of rejection and overt rebellion, my choice now is to pray for Insane Christians. Again, item four above, if employed fully, will clearly demonstrate to those Insane Christians that my peace is genuine and cradled in the love of Christ. Will such Insane Christians change? Who knows? That is not mine to worry about. Living a rich and full Christian life is my personal challenge, and one that should occupy enough of my time to rid any chance of my tendency to judge my fellow soldiers for the weapons they choose.

You may be wondering about now if, perhaps, I'm the insane one. Why do I feel so compelled to draft such a piece?

While I've taken some cheap shots at, perhaps, the genesis of my own Christianity, please appreciate that I'm simply trying to grow and to learn more. As I move forward, hold me accountable to these words. In fact, as a closing statement on this 'new definition' of Christianity, I argue back to myself that <u>this is not a new definition!</u> It's how Christ defined it some 2,000 years ago. This is really the *oldest* definition, with a dramatically changed perspective, that being focusing on *my personal relationship with Christ* first; realizing "who the good guys are," finding a church that fits for my style, and continuing to grow up as a Christian.

"Instead, speaking the truth in love, we will in all things grow up into him who is the head, that is, Christ. From him the whole body, joined and held together by every supporting ligament, grows and builds itself up in love, as each part does its work." (Eph. 4:15, 16)

No Excuses

The concept of Insanity may sound like an excuse for my leaving Christianity for more than two decades. It's time to come clean on this, as well.

First, there is no excuse for drifting from God. I'll be held accountable for this time, pure and simple. I was raised by two wonderful Christian parents who are, to this day, <u>the most brilliant examples of what it means to be true Christ followers.</u> They afforded me freedom to explore. They afforded me the ability to think and make decisions on my own, while holding steady to their own values and unconditional love. They truly are my life heroes.

So I offer the above as an analytical way of explaining how I drifted away, not as an excuse. You might say that I exploited God's Free Will gift to me. And that assessment would be correct.

Case in point would be Paul's letter to Timothy in his explanation of his journey. As you rewind in history, Paul was a really bad guy prior to him becoming a Christian. In 1 Timothy 1:15, we read in a letter written by Paul to Timothy.

"This is a faithful saying and worthy of acceptance, that Christ Jesus came into the world to save sinners, of whom I am chief." (NK JV)

Paul is not exaggerating here because before he became a Christian (Saul), his life was centered on killing off Christianity, literally and figuratively. He did much damage to the church, and he even killed a multitude of people just because they professed to follow Christ.

But Paul was not stymied by this checkered past. He rose above it and buried the past and moved on. You might say that he went from being the worst to the first in terms of having a huge impact on the growth of Christianity. He ended up authoring many books in the New Testament. He ditched his guilt trip, as well, and did not let his past paralyze his future. In this, I find huge hope.

In I Timothy 1:14, he writes, *"The grace of our Lord was exceedingly abundant."* (NKJV)

Grace was his answer to how God turned things around for him. Guilt was replaced by God's grace. And through God's grace, Paul became a tremendous servant of the Lord. Aside from grace, this would not have happened. Pure and simple.

"However, for this reason I obtained mercy, that in me first Jesus Christ might show all long suffering, as a pattern to those who are going to believe on Him for everlasting life." (1 Timothy 1:16)

I would claim the same thing that Paul so eloquently purports. I've been a failure, I've messed up big time and I have no excuse, yet by God's amazing Grace (and patience), I don't have to remain in a paralyzed spiritual status.

I have my parents to thank for leading me to Christ to begin with. Yet I have to reconcile with God those many years that I failed to follow Him. I have some lost time to make up. Which brings us here: to the greatest crossroads of my life, where chaos would bring clarity and piece everything together.

Chapter 3

The Bike Ride

It's a hot summer Friday evening in early August, and life is perfect. I am riding my new mountain bike (less than 200 miles on it) alongside my son in Fort Collins, Colorado.

We decide to go on a short fly fishing trip on the Poudre River, less than a half a mile from my son's home. While heading to the Poudre River, I make the decision to wear only my fishing cap without my helmet – the first time I have ever done this — since we are traveling such a short route to the river. Plus, I need the flip-down bill-glasses to tie on the No. 14 flies that we will use. Not to mention, the road is closed. There shouldn't be any traffic. This choice seems small. But it will end up changing my life.

Shorts, ball cap and my backpack, where crisscrossed inside are two backpack fly rods encased in sturdy 18-inch PVC tubes.

These fly rods will later save my back from being broken.

We had already postponed this fishing trip by a day, and this Friday evening, Aug. 3, 2007, made it even more special. No work tomorrow. Yippee! We can take our time, fish a while, go back home and watch a rerun of the "Survivorman: Arctic" episode. That is the plan.

If we were to have stayed on the river just 30 more seconds, none of this would have happened. This book would not have been written.

Had we made just one more cast, taken another sip of water or even just peddled back home at a slower rate, things would have remained absolutely perfect. Maybe. The issue is timing, being at the precise point in time where something happens to you that changes your life.

The Christian life is not some random series of events that simply happen. God controls everything, and I do not believe that God *creates* disasters. God allows the forces of His created nature, physics and energy to work (which He created), *and in some cases, bad things do happen.* This experience was going to happen, so the timing is perfect. Absolutely perfect. God knew this when I was born some 55 years ago.

To the Christ-believer, God never puts us through something we cannot endure. That's the theme of the book of Job. *How we handle* such issues can either be a spiritual growth experience or we can curse God and deny Him. In Job's case, he went from being the 2000 BC Donald Trump to a homeless sick man (most of his family dead) with leprosy, all in a matter of less than a few hours. (And I thought that I had a bad day!) Talk about perfect timing. How he handled it made all the difference.

"In all this, Job did not sin by charging God with wrongdoing." (Job 1:21)

In my case, out of perfect timing comes perfect chaos. Less than five minutes from my son's home, I vaguely recall my son Nate looking over his left shoulder and saying something about an approaching car. I vaguely recall some car in the distance approaching us. Nate says something to me. He reaches his left arm toward me as if to pull me over closer to him. It's his last attempt to change what had to happen. And then, our family policy of "parent always on the traffic side" pays off.

Ever since our children were old enough to walk, run or bike, our family policy was that the children stay on the inside lane. I remember one 3-mile run with my daughter when we were arguing about this rule. She lost the argument and ran on the inside. The concept behind the rule was simple: if someone gets hit, it's better if it's the older one. Plus, it's a parent's normal instinct to protect the babies. Just try to get between a mother and her bear cubs if you need more convincing!.

Other than the normal disregard for pedestrians or bikers, my 25 years of running and biking nearly every day never resulted in any significant accident. There were some close calls, but never any major accident.

That is until around 7:07 p.m. this Aug. 3, when a driver coming home from work — on a closed road — fails to see me and my son. The result: two broken legs, compound fractures of my right tibia and fibula, broken left foot, several broken ribs, a skull fracture, a concussion, brain bleeding, many scrapes and a totaled mountain bike. The fly rods in their sturdy PVC tubes inside my backpack probably saved my back from being broken. In fact, they made it through with only minor scratches (and have caught a few fish since!).

Of course, I don't know any of that right now. As my body lies, half-submerged, in a rain-filled gutter, tangled in its own broken limbs, I don't know anything.

My son leans over me crying. He is emotionally crushed. Helpless, but a problem solver.

He summons 911.

But I am not here.

Enter the Black Room. . .

Chapter 4

The Black Room

Nothing. Blackness. No pain. Spinning. Blanks. Big Blanks. Pain. Fear. Every emotion caving in simultaneously on fast forward, yet I am not aware of time. The steely taste in the back of my mouth is constant and growing. It gets worse. Blackly suspended somewhere, I think that I cannot think, something has taken control over me, and now I know it was this thing called shock. Shock was my mind's way of taking me out of the picture, knowing subconsciously that I did not want to know what the picture was. The big mirror in the back yard just received a brick.

Nevertheless, there seems to be an internal war going on inside my brain. The conscious mind fights to regain control, to take over from the shock. So in this battle, memory fragments are left strewn on the battlefield of control. My head is beyond hurting. My mind has been hit. Slight and bright noisy lights flash, and my spinning mind continues. I am still not aware of time, yet time seems to stop, then race forward like a bolt of electricity. Things are shocking me. Now, everything stops, and I'm wondering if my heart will. I actually don't care. I fear the fear. Time seems to be the walls inside this black room, and the walls seem to be getting smaller. It's as if things are closing in on me in the dark. I am very afraid. And I taste it throughout my body.

I'm so messed up that my mind won't allow me to realize this condition. Confusion and torment between trying to be "normal" and shock still rage on. The heat of summer seems to make me carsick in the back of what I later realize to be an ambulance. I think I vomit somewhere. Some dark black-blue uniformed people are shuffling in the ambulance, fighting for balance against the vehicle's speed and turning motions, which somehow I am OK with. I must be strapped into something. Red shards of light pierce the darkness of wherever I am.

There are rattling noises of equipment, bottles and other things that are being plugged into me. It is hot. Everything is bloody, and the blood seems to be like hot glue on fire deep inside within many places on my body. What little I can remember seeing is from my right eye, as the other is in trouble somehow, which now is another problem that bothers my mind.

Something is really wrong with my legs and my head. It's almost pointless to breathe. I am very hot. Everything is black and dark, except for the blasts of intense lights flashing constantly if I try and open my left eye. I know it's dark out and the sun must have set. That's my only sense of time. My left eye doesn't work. Caked mud, dirt, blood and sweat are lathered over me like half-dried, ignited glue.

Blasting into the ER, my left eye can see yellow shreds of bright white and yellowish blurry lights with many, many people doing things to me, not asking me questions, some of them looking afraid. Should I be afraid? The taste in my mouth is now something different, and these people are now trying to save my life. I realize this but don't care. The more I care, the less I can do. Caring doesn't seem to work. It's the first time in my life that I have felt 100% out of control.

All of the sudden I care a whole lot. I'm frightened. Where is my son? What happened to him? Where is my daughter? Where is my wife? Where am I and what happened? I think I see my wife and she's crying. I think my wife signs some papers. She is afraid. She looks like love. She is clearly disturbed and crying, I think.

I don't know what to say and cannot speak because something is in my mouth and these people have taken over my entire life with machines, tubes, needles, things that snap, all sorts of technology. The best technology is running noisily with cables, cameras, screens and beeping sounds. Yet I can feel the love of my family, and those fragments feel good.

More whiteness fills something in the room and my body is motionless from within, yet violently being manipulated from without. I don't know what is happening. I think something bad has happened to me, but when and where? I am extremely confused and feeling sick, but not the type of sickness like the flu. Some sick feeling, like things are really messed up somewhere in my body, but I don't know where. I know something is wrong with my legs. Very wrong.

What little I can feel, my legs are white hot. My head is dizzy and my teeth are bent. I am afraid it is really bad. I hear some familiar voices and then realize I need to get in control of this situation. Panic now sets in. I must get out. I must regain control of this situation. I am OK. Let me up! Blackness now enshrouds what slight sliver of light that I was seeing. Morphine is coursing through my body, yet it only helps for a bit. Isn't this what they do to fatally wounded soldiers on the battlefield before they die, I think? I wish that I didn't know this fact. I realize that I am thinking and it makes me more afraid.

The white turns to yellow and is engulfed by gray and finally total blackness envelopes my being with a loud ringing in my ears. The steely taste is constant. Inside this blackness is me, alone with my mind, as the only thing left that I can barely control, and I am afraid that I am also going to lose control of this last fragment of reality.

This is really happening and there's nothing I can do to control it. But I fight for control in my mind. There is a war going on in my head with large bombs exploding constantly with intense pain. When will this war end?

I am now facing my own spirit, fighting for control, yet losing on all accounts. I am at a specific point in my mind where I am alone, yet almost audibly hearing another person. It is like being in a totally dark room, not being able to feel anything, talking to someone in that room while knowing that something really bad is going on. The walls in the black room have stopped moving in on me. I am somewhat relieved of this. What that person said made me even more crazy and confused. Then gradually, from chaos comes perfection. We have a conversation that I vividly recall.

In this blackness, there are now no visible signs of life or people, yet I feel tugging, pulling and jerking of my body. I drift into and out of the black room. I am totally alone with God. I think I am moving toward the surgery room. I am being wheeled in the bed, occasionally seeing tubes, feeling my arms being manipulated and many people hovering over me doing things that I don't understand. They are continually talking to each other and keep looking at my face, but not for long durations. Just quick glances, then back to whatever they were doing. Concerned and intentional work, clearly not in their daily routine, I can tell that. Not in a chaotic way, I have a feeling that they may know what they are doing. Do I have any choice?

At first I think I'm talking to myself. In the black room that other person seems to be back. Then I realize it is God, my Creator, Jesus Christ and The Holy Spirit. This is The Trinity and me. So I guess there are four people in the black room, yet it seems like just two: me and God. The Trinity now makes perfect sense! We are trying to make sense out of all of this, but we as a team cannot. God doesn't like this any more than I do, but He is there. He's worried about my trust in Him. I can tell this.

Then there is a decision that is given to me: "You can either relax or let me take control, or try and do it yourself. Furthermore, you've already tried to 'fix' this over the past hour and half, and look how far it's gotten you. You are a mess, and this time you can't do anything about it. Accept the fact that you are out of your own control. You are not in control, and the more that you try and fight this, the worse it's going to get. Your only control now is to relax and give up control. Let these guys do their job. Trust me."

I know, finally, that this is beyond what I can fix. The war in my spirit is over. The battle is over. I have to surrender. In the black room, we also agree that it is OK if I need to leave this world, and in fact, it may be the easiest way out of this blind-black room. There is no bright light or anything that you hear about near-death experiences, even though this is precisely where I am. In fact, the black room is where I finally start to feel better, knowing that God has me. He is on the battlefield! I finally start trusting Him.

The discussion around me dying seems to be rejected right away. So we don't dwell on that too long. I am told that "this is not going to kill you." Once I know this fact from God, it is much easier to relax. I realize that maybe I had been fighting for my life, and when I didn't have to worry about that particular fight, things get a lot less tense. In fact, I recall hearing myself take this advice and say, "OK, kick back and let's relax." (I always speak in the plural person to myself.)

As soon as I give it up — give up trying to control — and relax in God's arms, I wake up, kind of, piecing together the images of many family members, friends, doctors, nurses and people that I don't even know. Everyone looks tired and worn out. They look like angels from Heaven. Tired angels.

I am out for maybe four or six hours but it seems like only a few minutes. Did I have several hours of surgery? I have no clue. But I remind myself about the decision that the only control I had was to give up control and let God have it. It feels like a huge burden is taken from me. I can actually relax, in some crazy manner, and allow people to do what they need to do and what they are trained to do.

This probably saves my life.

"Don't let this throw you. You trust God, don't you? Trust me. There is plenty of room for you in my Father's home. If that weren't so, would I have told you that I'm on my way to get a room ready for you? And if I'm on my way to get your room ready, I'll come back and get you so you can live where I live." (John 14:1, The Message)

The four or five days following are littered with peculiar dreams (probably from the morphine), stupid decisions that never material-ized (like "I'm going to get up and get my computer") and feeling the presence of the amazing love of my family.

I discover that my son is OK. It injects into me thankfulness and peace.

"Frog, I prayed for a miracle during the accident, and if you are reading this my miracle prayer was undoubtedly answered. We are going to have a long road to recovery, but we will be with you and God will be with us. We will learn a lot from this and we will go to Canada next year and it will be twice as nice. I love you higher than the highest mountain and deeper than the deepest sea."

— From Nathan

My daughter sleeps right next to me for at least three or four days, never leaving. So does my son, although he is still under severe shock, having witnessed all of what I cannot piece together. People try to explain to me what happened, and I am surprised. My daughter starts a journal where people can write their thoughts, feelings and prayers.

My wife's love goes beyond worrying about me to reminding me of what we had plans to do: the mission work in Africa. This gives me a surge of energy thinking that if she's still thinking of her trip, then I must be ok! Her vision never waivers, even in the wake of me almost dying!

In her words, "I must go through the valleys to stand upon the mountain of God."

She and my daughter are scheduled to leave for Uganda in one week. This whole ordeal now seems to interrupt plans and the scheduled mission trip. Will they have to cancel the trip?

My children-in-laws hold my hands, flood me with prayers and stop their lives to help save mine. At some point, they tell me what had happened, and this time I can accept it. And I begin to see the things that saved my life:

My son pulled me toward him right before impact. Even he doesn't recall the specific details. But I know it saved my life.

My son ran to my body heap which was thrown some 50 feet, landing on my face in a mud-filled gutter on this road that was closed for construction. He called 911 for help. (He told me that I tried to sit up on the curb. How ridiculous, with bones poking out of my right leg!) That saved my life.

My wife came immediately to my side and initiated worldwide prayers from literally thousands of people. My vague recollection was that she was afraid, very afraid. But I saw love in her that gave me life. She gave me the will to live. That saved my life.

My daughter slept right next to me, holding my hand in the dark and lonely nights. During one of those nights, she wrote:

I fade awake, eyes dry from the stale hospital air.
I hear you murmur in your sleep,
A baby, my daddy, you're wrapped in white cotton sheet.
I fade to sleep on the wooden chair to your left,
I won't leave you.
Now you fade awake, eyes swollen and puffy but still the most
*   beautiful blue,*
Scanning the room in curiosity.
You can't see me but you must feel me,
As you fade back to sleep.
I fade awake now.
We're on a shared teeter-totter of consciousness.
I hear you snore and I smile, never happier to hear that sound.
The silly source of fights when I was a teenager.
I am older, so are you,
But that snore still hasn't changed.
I love that snore.
I fade into a dream,
You take my place in the awakeness.
Your hands crawl up your swollen face and clasp the top of
*   your bald head.*
The same shiny bald head that got sunburned from golfing
*   too much.*
It's bloody today, but I think your hair looks nicely orderly,
What hair you have.
It'll keep your precious head warm.
You chase down another snore into dreamland.
I fade awake, cheek smushed
On a beige wall.
Not even stale white.

I scan the hospital room in approval.
Not that bad of a place.
You shift and your bed creaks, and although I can tell your
  broken legs hurt, you are moving,
And that is beautiful.
Your tiny shift looks like a ballroom dance to your
  daughter's eyes,
Which now must fall into the weight of these hefty lids.
You wake up with a jump, not fearful, but excited.
Not knowing the details but knowing where your strength
  comes from.
You don't feel strong right now, but you and I know you are.
I wake up and find you awake.
I take a breath and so do you.
You sigh and I stand up at your left shoulder.
"What mess I am," you say.
"But I am alive."

Aimee allowed me to have these idiotic dreams and even talked to me about them. She acted like they were real. She played along. This helped me since I was certain that these dreams were reality. One dream that I vividly remember was that I thought I was on hole nine of some fancy golf course and needed to inform the rest of my foursome that my legs hurt and I couldn't play the rest of the nine holes. I actually tried to convince people that I couldn't finish. I was trying to locate the golf cart. My daughter played along, until she finally brought me to reality in a very gentle way. Her laughter gave me huge volumes of strength because I figured if she was having a good time, then I must be OK. That saved my life.

Also, there were prayers from literally around the world.

"I got every Christ-follower I know praying for you, my friend. I'll tell you this when I see you, but I'm writing it down here, too. I've decided to name my fly rod 'Frog' because I've caught a lot of fish with it, it's a little banged up and I know I'm going to catch a lot more fish with it in the future. I love you, brother." — From Wayne, my best fishing buddy

My wife rounded up prayers from Africa, through Europe and here in the states. People got on their knees for me. <u>Our extended African family prayed for a solid day</u>.

A text from our friends, Marcel and Benson, in Africa read: "Soon we will enter a new life without sorrows and problems only singing and praising. ... Satan will be ashamed. We serve a living God. I believe in miracles. Frog is gonna be alright...We're with and many angels from God are there around you... I and my group of friends are praying. Be strong; we are on our knees praying."

My mom and dad cried to God. A phone call from my sister: "Very concerned, praying continually...deepest love sent."

These prayers saved my life.

It was not my time. I realized this early on when I was alone in the black room with God. I guess God wasn't ready for me quite yet. He saved my life as well as my soul.

"So do not fear, for I am with you; do not be dismayed, for I am your God. I will strengthen you and help you; I will uphold you with my righteous right hand." (Isaiah 41:10)

I am in ICU for about a week. Normally, I'm not that popular of a guy, but I grow shocked by the continual flood of people stopping by, delivering food, flowers and books, and each one prays with me. I am alive and they all are glad.

I hear of other nearby ICU patients not so "lucky" as I am, and it builds perspective. I hear of at least one who passes away. A guy enters the next room after a motorcycle accident and dies after two days. I hear of other people dying in rooms close by.

In my room, there is never one moment where I am alone. God is even relieved. I can tell this.

As the days pass in ICU, my prognosis becomes better and the brain swelling and bleeding subsides. I continue piecing together what happened.

Even though my left eye is still pretty blurry, it is not badly damaged. In seeing my son, holding his hand and feeling his tender touch, rebirths our life relationship. It's something that I will never be able to explain. The bond between my family and my loving children-in-laws grows deep. Some people come to see me who I have not seen in years. Our church is constantly at the ready, offering and providing anything, any time, constantly for my family. People demonstrate true Christian love and compassion. The love runs deep. <u>This is Christianity in action.</u>

"You are moving around a little and I can tell you have a lot of pain. You reached your hand up to the sky and I stood behind you. I asked God, 'How many angels can you fit in this room to watch over my dad?' I expected to hear 'all the angels in the world' but he said, 'I only need just one.' I smiled." — From Nathan

Chapter 5

From ICU to Rehab

W hile I stay in ICU, my friends and family camp out in a visitor lounge. They set up a gaming table of sorts, bring in movies and take over the room. They call it the "central command post," through which people can organize work to be done and plan out how to help me. It becomes the nerve center for this disaster control. Our church brings in food, and I am told it is pretty amazing. Since I never could venture into the "central command post," I never had the chance to eat any of the fine food until later on when other's brought food to my house.

I never venture into this room, since I am confined to the bed and it is on a different level across the hospital.

Things are still blurry, but I think it's around the fourth day in ICU. The concussion seems to be healing enough to allow me to start regaining an overall picture and consciousness. They conduct cognitive tests and I pass them all with flying colors. That builds my confidence. The morphine is no longer needed, and my weird dreams stop. My family takes me on rolls out around my wing of the hospital, and eventually even outside where I can see the beautiful Colorado Rocky Mountains. My legs are there, but pretty much useless. I begin to learn how to "transfer" myself from the bed to the wheelchair. This will become a critical part of my next few months.

Finally, it is time for me to move out of ICU. Normal life is starting to return to some semblance of sanity, at least from an intensive care perspective. It is a blessing when the nurse starts to arrange an ambulance for me to relocate to the rehab hospital in Fort Collins. My mind is relieved. I never thought I'd ever look forward to going to a Rehab Unit! This was better than graduating from college!

But making the move is no small task, since our family has been camped out for almost a week. Not to mention the presents, books, flowers and computer equipment. I have no clue how we move from ICU to rehab; the family takes care of the details.

I'll never forget the ambulance ride to the rehab hospital. This ride is unlike the first one, in that I remember everything, I feel alive and it isn't dark and scary. My daughter makes the trip with me and takes pictures en-route. We are smiling and happy. Life *is* going to continue.

"Your eyes are looking at me. They're trying to tell me something. They're asking and pleading. You want to know what I'm thinking. You want to know how this miracle has transformed me. I can tell you this: Your pain is not in vain. This is a cross roads. I get it. I get so much now that I didn't get before. I'm too exhausted to find the words right now. I want to desperately tell you everything. But my eyes are looking at you. They're trying to tell you something. They want to tell you life will be OK. They want to tell you what I now know. I love you. I am feeling 'sane.' Surprisingly sane." — From Aimee

I arrive at the rehab hospital on a Saturday and set up camp in what resembles a normal hospital room, compared with the ICU room, which was tangled with cords and special machines and had windows instead of walls to allow for constant supervision. I welcome the stale while walls and simplicity of my new home because they symbolize recovery, not just survival.

The rehab hospital is full of friendly and helpful personnel. I feel welcomed, but realize that I still am broken and in need of some serious work. My mind now focuses on the challenges ahead, and the stress sets in. Somehow, some day, I realize I'm supposed to learn to walk again.

It's Saturday, and we're having a family meeting about my wife and daughter's trip to Africa, happening now in a matter of days. This is a critical decision and stressful. The family feels torn between whether to stay and show support for me or to continue with the extensively-planned humanitarian trip. The airplane tickets could not be refunded and the people in Africa, while supportively understood the gravity of my situation, still wanted to see my wife and daughter. Meanwhile, people were dying of malaria.

The family meeting was emotional, with some people feeling that the continuation of the trip was completely insensitive, and others feeling that it should proceed; that it would send a message that life was going on, and that I would recover. We'd had other high-stress family meetings before, and we'd learned to let each person listen patiently and keep the order civil and respectful.

After several hours of listening and discussing, I made the decision that Beth and Aimee simply *must go*. The rationale was simple: Since I was going to be in the hospital for at least another two weeks, they really couldn't do any more directly to help my recovery. It was also a matter of keeping to our plans and mission to keep Think Humanity going. The mission would suffer if we postponed.

After making a decision, the family is united and supports it 100 percent. My wife and daughter say their goodbyes. We pray. And then they leave for Africa.

We all are solidly confident in this tough decision, and God blesses it as a result. My wife and daughter develop contacts with our extended African family, resulting in the establishment of a malaria-eradication project called Meds and Nets, and eventually the nonprofit organization called Think Humanity. The girls get under way the plans for an orphanage in the refugee settlement, as well as setting up the first date for an event called MaNdate, where more than 700 insecticide-treated nets will be distributed.

Had they balked at taking this trip, the progress would have been stymied, and if those 700 nets had not been distributed, more lives would have been lost from the dreaded malaria. Had they not made the trip, it would have stymied the growth of Think Humanity and thwarted the literal saving of lives in Africa. My life had been saved, and it was now our time to let God take me in his hands so my family could help save more lives.

God is in control, and once again our trust is tested.

The blow-out

Around the second day in the rehab hospital, I am feeling pretty good and visit the rehab gym in my new wheelchair. I actually feel quite feisty and tough! I am still trying to figure out how to get around, get in and out of the wheelchair, use the elevated potty chair, take showers with plastic bags tied around my legs and how to do all of the basic functions that we normally take for granted.

At any rate, I venture into the gym along with a physical therapist who is substituting a shift for my regular one. This therapist seems quite aggressive and indicates that I need to "get the bad (explicit) out of my head and the good (explicit) in." Having never been in rehab before, and being an aggressive type-A person myself, I erroneously listen to him. While we are in the gym, he asks me to do some leg exercises. Note that I had two leg surgeries less than one week prior. I am in partial casts with pins still sticking out of my left foot. The therapist tells me to stand, so I stand. He tells me to sit. I sit.

When I sit down, he fails to tell me to keep my left knee straight, nor does he help me. When I sit down on the wheelchair, I feel an explosion in my left knee. The pain is incredible. Once again, the fire in my left knee is back, except this time, I am completely cognizant of what's going on, and I am worried that this is going to require more surgery.

I know I did something terribly bad. I am in excruciating pain as the therapist wheels me back to my room and into my bed. Since it is the weekend, my orthopedic doctor is out and can't see me until Monday.

These next hours, the pain meds even fail to work and my mental condition is depleted. I dread that doctor visit since I am afraid that it will require more surgery. My son is also stressing over this, and knows what happened. My son is angry at the substitute therapist and has aggressive discussions with the doctors in the rehab unit.

The following Monday morning, my orthopedic doctor finally comes in, takes X-rays and sticks a hypodermic needle into my ballooned knee, draining more than 12 ounces of fluid. This now trumps the other pains, becoming the most painful experience of the entire ordeal. I am awake and watching. I see the fluid pour into the hypodermic needle reservoir, and I cry while clutching each side of the bedrail with a death grip. The doctor astutely looks at the fluid and comments gingerly that he's glad that there's not that much blood. I guess I am glad, too.

After more X-rays, his prognosis is that more surgery will be required. He explains that the knee cap rewiring blew apart when I sat down and bent it too far. My son and I cannot believe our ears. Another setback and huge disappointment. And my wife and daughter are already in the air, flying to Africa. We pray and give it again to the Lord.

Fortunately, the doctor is able to expedite the surgery within two days. During this waiting time, my spirit sinks and my son and his wife keep me going. They bring me food and stay the nights with me, sleeping in chairs.

After surgery number three, I am back in my room. My son and daughter-in-law are by my side continually. I hate the long nights, so they take turns being with me, sleeping in a chair and then dragging into their jobs the next morning somehow. Lindsey manages all of my needed equipment, ranging from a brand new wheelchair to a home potty chair. She does everything she can. She handles 100% of everything, taking the entire burden.

Lindsey is a special angel that God sends to me. She becomes my companion. We talk about nothing, which means everything, and she manages to work via her laptop while I watch TV and try to log on to my work and catch up on the thousands of e-mail piling up. I call up my boss and have a brief meeting for some expenditure approvals. He didn't argue about anything during that meeting!

Later, when I will return to my house, Lindsey will come over many days and affectionately call our house the "The Heckel Home Corporate Office Tower," where we both will work remotely.

But even today in the hospital, her being there means so much to me. She takes time out of her day to fetch me a soda. She wheels me around outside for a bit. She puts her work on hold. It is a sacrifice that helps me much. She becomes my best friend. We joke and make fun of the weird people that are taking care of me.

Over the next two weeks, I proceed through the schedule of Rehab, attend daily rehab exercise classes, eat to regain my 30 lost pounds and learn to tackle the things that non-handicapped people take for granted; showering, eating, getting in and out of bed, reaching for something across the room and coping with my new limitations. Taking a shower involved my son helping me to put my legs into plastic bags, getting out of the bed and onto the wheel chair, then wheeling down to the shower, transferring myself to the shower seat, then managing to wash the best I could. Nathan helped in all of this and it took over an hour each day. I quickly learn how to navigate in a wheel chair and build up my upper body by taking laps around the rehab section of the hospital. I gained a whole new perspective of people with handicaps.

I learn a lot through this process and finally the day comes when I get to leave for my home some 20 days later. Lindsey, my angel, replicated a hospital room in the lower floor of our house. Our church and my son constructed wheel-chair ramps so that I could get around. I even resumed part-time working from home.

I visited my office, but the layout of the office was not designed for a handicapped person. I also needed a lot of bed-time rest and found that the normal volume of stress was intolerable coupled with my physical handicapped condition. Home nurses came and went on a daily basis. Going to the grocery store was a huge deal. I couldn't drive but just the simple act of getting into and out of the car took over 10 minutes. My driver, my wife, was ever so patient and gracious. She never complained about managing the situation and always managed to get me a Starbucks.

But I had a lot of time on my hands. There's only so much boring day-time TV one can consume and I hit that limit in short order! Given that I had time on my hands, I read, studied God's Word and began this book. My daughter (editor of this book) told me, to "write and just start putting things in my head and heart down on paper." One of the glaring and needed chapters of this book was a chapter entitled "Lessons Learned." What was I learning from all of this? What was God saying? What important life lessons should I take away from all of this? That leads us into the next chapter...

Chapter 6

Lessons Learned

L essons learned. That sounds like I have it all figured out, but that is far from reality. I still have lingering questions, a lot of anger and much confusion. While I've regained much of my physical abilities (~75%), the challenge to move on, to adapt and to learn challenged me.

Growth is a process, and sometimes the bones heal quicker than the spirit. There's also a huge difference between *learning* and *applying*. In college, I learned calculus (and received straight A's in a topic that required me to accept some axioms, and then regurgitate on tests). That *learning process* was not immediately applied to my corporate life until many years later, when things started to tie together. A function (back to calculus) started to take on meaning, and I could *start to apply* what I learned many years later. Now some of those college classes that were, at the time, seemingly useless start to take form, fit together nicely and become applicable to much of my work. I may be regarded as a slower learned, or maybe a slower applier.

While I can talk about the things that I've *learned* as a result of the accident, it does not mean that I have mastered *the application of those lessons*. In fact, as I write this, I am challenged myself to listen to my words and really apply them to my life. I pray daily that my wisdom will grow and that what I've put down here will become rock solid in my life.

As for now, I don't have any keen insight more than the next guy, and I don't have it all figured out. In some cases, I have even more questions than before. The Christian life is a constant battle, one that is not easy and one that is always challenged.

Entering into my senior years, it takes a lot more convincing to change my mind. It takes more logic, more thinking, more weighing situations versus my life experiences and much more faith. So maybe the lessons are written more to me than to anyone else. I tend to listen to myself more than others anyway, so there you go!

Note to self: Listen to what you are saying, Jim. Apply these lessons. Have more hope, have more faith. Listen to God! He's speaking much more than you are hearing!

Lesson one: It wasn't *my* accident.

To this day, I have many people ask me, "How are you doing after your accident?" The implication is that it only impacted me. While they mean well, I've learned that too many times we tend to connect accidents with only the person directly involved. In my case, since I was the one physically injured, then it was "my accident."

In appreciation of the cascading stress that it placed on my friends and family, I now refer to this as *the* accident. Sure, I was a main participant in the accident. Yet it impacted lives that span way beyond simply mine. In fact, to a large extent, the accident blew through other people's lives even more so than mine. It disrupted people's work, re-commanded their time, created huge amounts of stress and took over their control the instant that it happened.

Of particular note is my son, Nathan.

Most people ask Nathan, "How's your dad doing?" But the real question should be, "How's the family doing?" And "How are you doing, Nathan?" While it truly was a blessing to me that Nathan was not injured and I was, in a way, this is a selfish attitude. Let me explain.

Most parents would agree that if they were asked to put up their life for their child, they'd do this in a flash. No thinking involved. Of course, I'd give up my life for my child. This is rooted in a deep-seated love that parents have for their children. This is, indeed, admirable. (My chest is puffed out presently!)

Back to the accident, however, I maintain that my son Nathan went through much more than I did. (My chest is no longer puffed out.) Physical injuries are tough, but emotional injuries are even tougher. Nathan had to witness the entire ordeal, watch his father be hit by a car doing more than 35 miles per hour and then run to his (hopeful) rescue. Seeing this with no shock (unlike me, where shock took over control) placed Nathan in probably the most stressful situation imaginable. In fact, Nathan said that he had already grieved my death, since he really didn't know if I would make it. The sheer roller-coaster ride from surprise to fear to the need to solve a problem to helplessness in a matter of minutes was much more stressful than being injured, medicated and treated. I maintain to this day that he was the unsung hero and endured more psychological pain and suffering than I did.

As time moved on, people started to figure this out, however, and paid some attention to him. And I started to think about the family bike riding policy of the parent being on the outside. It suddenly sounded a bit selfish. Did I really wish to place myself in harm's way because of love, or was it because I would rather endure the physical pain versus the emotional torture of seeing my child hurt? It's a question that bothers me.

And if it bothers me to have to witness my child being hurt, then it brings into perspective the first huge lesson.

God gave up His only son to *die* for me. Christ came to Earth with one intention: to be our hope of salvation. He and the Father God knew that this was going to happen. God had to endure 33 years of stress while Jesus was alive, knowing that His will needed to be accomplished through the death and resurrection of Jesus. Jesus knew all along of his torturous and required crucifixion.

The Bible tells us that Christ experienced life just like we do and felt the same way that we feel. Jesus had stress in His Holy life. And the night before His crucifixion must have been beyond what we can imagine as stress, since He sweat drops of blood. How amazing. The lesson learned is the amazing love that God has for us to allow His only son to die for a person like me. This truly is beyond my ability to imagine. I don't have that type of love to give up my son for another's life.

So when Nathan endured the stress of seeing his father being thrown around like a rag doll, think of the comparison that God went through when He sent Jesus to Earth, knowing that Jesus would have to endure the most violent torture and be crucified for the sins of mankind. But God did this.

It is undeniable. Christ changed everything. If you are reading this and you don't believe in Jesus, I simply ask you to ponder the question, "Who was Jesus?" If you answer the question by rationalizing that Jesus was just another prophet, then why does the entire world make such a fuss over Jesus? Why do we take Jesus' name in vain and not the other prophets? Why is there this thing called Christmas that literally transforms the world into a season of peace and giving? And it is quite undeniable the historic context from which the Christmas Holiday originated. Why is there life and how did it all just happen? Where did the notion of good and bad come from?

The more that I read about the Big Bang Theory, the more that it seems to support Creationism. This is called Intelligent Design Theory. Out of nothing came something. And where did nothing come from? If you continue down this line of reasoning to the point where simple energy is the genesis of the Big Bang, then what is this energy? Where did this energy come from?

Does molecular organization come from simple randomness of infinite combinations and permutations? This is statistically irrational! What about the theory of entropy: things left unattended gravitate toward a state of un-organization? Ice (neatly packed molecules) turns into water (less organized molecules) and finally into vapor (totally unorganized atoms). Just leave your house unattended for a week holiday, and you'll come back to a house that is dusty and in need of cleaning. Peeling it back further, one has to ultimately come to the point where something created something.

These are some of the things that came to my mind while I sat alone after the accident, watching the sun rise and simply appreciating this thing called life. Who grants life? It is even ironic that we call the sun the "sun," since it sounds exactly like the Son, who is the Light of the world and in Him there is no darkness. We cannot stare at the sun else we'll burn the retina in our eye and become blind. In the Old Testament when people tried to face God, they were blinded. I'm not saying that God is the sun, only being sensitive to the laws of nature — the perfect way that Earth is orchestrated — and then resolving this mystery through a solidified faith in God the Father, Jesus the Son and the Holy Spirit. The Trinity! At some point, some faith in something has to occur; else we are simply random people roaming in a random world. And if that is the case, then there cannot exist any purpose in one's life. It simply makes no sense.

Remember back in the Black Room? At first I thought that there were four people in the room, and then all of the sudden the Trinity made perfect sense. At least this is where I put my head at night on the pillow, and it feels quite nice.

Which brings us back to the objective this book: To give honor and glory to Jesus Christ. To take what some may call a bad experience and to turn it into a positive experience...

In Philippians 4, we read:

"Rejoice greatly in the Lord that at last you have renewed your concern for me. Indeed, you have been concerned, but you had no opportunity to show it. I am not saying this because I am in need, for I have learned to be content whatever the circumstances. I know what it is to be in need, and I know what it is to have plenty. I have learned the secret of being content in any and every situation, whether well fed or hungry, whether living in plenty or in want. I can do everything through him who gives me strength."

If you're not a Christian, consider God. Here's an assignment: Some time when you have 20 minutes, get alone. This may be a quiet spot in your home or laying out on the lawn. But get alone and simply ask God to reveal Himself to you. Don't expect a lightning bolt to zip across the sky, necessarily (although it could happen!). Ask God to help you understand who He really is.

Then listen. Be open. If you pride yourself in open-mindedness, then have a truly open mind. How open is your mind? How open is your heart? And also then consider who this person Jesus is. Historically, what person ever had such an impact on the world? Give yourself some time to do this. For some people, it happens instantly, while for others, it takes more time. Allow God to speak to you. He will if you ask. Is your mind open or closed to this idea? And you don't have to be fancy in your words. Just talk to Him.

If you're already a Christian, and you have accepted Christ as your savior, answer the following question: Have you given your life to Christ?

It is one thing to give your heart to Christ, and Christians know that this grants us eternal life in heaven with God, but the next level is to give your life to Christ. When Jesus happened on Peter and James on the Sea of Galilee (they were fishermen by trade), He told them to leave their work and He would teach them to be "fishers of men." (Mark Chapters 3-5). Can you imagine James going home that evening and telling his wife, "Hey, I quit my job today; I'm going to follow Christ." To which she probably thought (as any normal rational human would), "OK, James, but how are we going to eat?" I'm not suggesting pulling the plug on work, becoming an independent isolationist and moving into the hills to become "at one with nature." What I am challenging you – and I, especially — is to consider what it means to give your entire life to Christ.

I am trying to deal with this right now while writing this. And during my quiet rehab time alone on those long summer afternoons in the wheelchair, God was with me, just like during the time in the Black Room. He is with you right now, and He is with me right now, helping me write this.

I know that He speaks to us more than we typically chose to hear. And during tough times, He is the one we seek. Why don't we seek Him during the good times, as well? The next time that you're in the grocery store, and you see all of the abundant supplies of food and life, give thanks to God. The next time you're reading a book (maybe this one) relaxing, stop and give thanks to God for your life, your eyes, your brain and the fact that Jesus died for you. Consider the question: "Have I given my *life* to Christ, as well as my heart?"

Lesson two: "Challenges in life don't arise haphazardly, no matter how accidental or coincidental they may seem." They only arrive when you're ready for them. ... "Ready to grow, overcome and be more than who you were before they arrived."

That's what my daughter, Aimee, wrote on a piece of paper she gave to me. She was quoting Mike Dooley, from "Notes from the Universe."

For the Christmas after the accident, my creative daughter gave me what she called a "thought box." This was a brightly colored green and glass box packed full of thoughts, one for each day of the year. Some thoughts are scripture verses, some quotations and others are her words.

Lesson No. 2 is one of those thoughts. Aimee had a tough year 2007, with other problems in addition to the accident. She called 2007 a season of growth. The Bible speaks of how parents will learn much from their children in Proverbs 15:20: *"A wise son"* – or daughter – *"brings joy to his father."* And so it goes, me learning much from my children, with a sense of joy.

This lesson is a big one. After coming home from the hospital, my mother gave me a book entitled <u>Let God be God</u>, by the late Ray C. Stedman. She had the book for several years and finally decided to give it to me, knowing that I'd have some time to read during my rehab. It is an expository work on the Book of Job. I consumed — not simply read — this book. In fact, after consuming the book, its binding was in such bad shape (from taking notes, underlining things and digging into it) that I had to put it into a two-ring binder.

The lesson from reading this book is captured in the essence of challenges in life, which do not arise haphazardly, no matter how accidental or coincidental they may seem. They only arrive when you're ready for them. "When you are ready to grow, overcome and be more than who you were before they arrived," as the quote goes.

Rewind to around 2000 BC. The Donald Trump-equivalent of the time was a man named Job who lived in the country of Uz. In less than 24 hours, he endured the death of his children, his wife left him, he went bankrupt and then got leprosy. Talk about a bad day! Since Job was a well known man, he had three so-called friends visit him to consul him and see how he was doing (much like visitors in a hospital). These three men didn't really help Job grow; rather, they challenged Job to curse God and die. The book goes through this very lengthy debate in gory detail. But Job never caved.

During his rehab time, Job had time to think about things. Why did God allow one of His best believers to endure such pain and torture?

The answer may be that God had confidence in Job. God knew that Job would be a better man after having gone through such calamity. And in the end, as you know, Job gets to hear from God, and Job's faith grows exponentially. In fact, at the end of the story, Job is better off than before, being blessed with more children and riches than he had before.

The lessons here are so many, it's hard to even categorize them, but let me attempt. I break them down into four pieces:

A) Since God created everything, including the laws of physics and nature, God doesn't always *stop* catastrophes, accidents, deaths, sickness and what we call bad events in life.

God most certainly *could* control events, so His believers would never have a bad day. But God shows no partiality and loves everyone the same. If He were to grant only good things to His believers, then it would defeat His plan to give man free will.

Instead, He wants to see our faith. For example, if when you became a Christian, life became perfect, then how much faith would it take for people to turn to Christ? It would be a simple logical act to "fix" life. Free will requires faith. Hebrews 11:1 defines Faith as *"being sure of what we hope for and certain of what we do not see."* God gave us a mind with free will to choose. And He wants us to demonstrate faith in Him, not simply to make a logical choice. How much faith would it take to simply make a logic choice?

B) When God *allows* bad things to happen to Christians, He may be demonstrating that He has confidence in a person's faith.

Recall the Job situation. God and Satan were in an argument and Satan threw down the challenge: "Give me your best guy, and

I'll break him!" To which God replied, "OK, you can mess with Job, so long as you don't take his life." God wins, Satan loses. Good trumps evil.

This is a tough one to understand (for me, at least), and in a way it sounds a bit arrogant. But God knows that through trials and tests, if we place our faith in Him, we will grow, and our faith will expand.

The best quarterbacks in the NFL occasionally throw an interception. Occasionally, they get sacked. How they handle those situations makes them become either better or worse. The process by which we become stronger involves tearing down the muscles, thereby allowing them to grow new cells that are even stronger. The same physical laws of muscle building apply to our spiritual lives, as well.

James 1:2-4 says, *"Consider it pure joy, my brothers, whenever you face trials of many kinds, because you know that the testing of your faith develops perseverance. Perseverance must finish its work so that you may be mature and complete, not lacking anything."*

C) **God never puts His children through more than they can endure**.

Job was the acid test of this, and we see that in the end, Job is victorious. The critical thing here is that during the tough times, we must seek out God even more, stay in His Word, build on our trust and talk to Him a lot.

During my rehab, I was alone a lot. I had time to really sort things out, lying awake at night, wondering, "Why me?" And during those quiet times, God's presence did not completely eradicate my physical loneliness, but it gave me peace. It gave me a new appreciation that God is not finished with my time on this planet. It gave me hope that in some way, God can use me. Hence, the reason I write.

D) **In the Christian life "coincidences" are actually "God-cidences."**

Each Wednesday morning, my son and I attend a Bible study. It's held at 7 a.m. at a local Perkins Restaurant, and this Bible study group has been around for more than 20 years. The group is non-denominational and is a mixture of Christian people who are simply trying to learn more about Christ. In essence, it's epitomizes my 'new' definition of Christianity. During one of the early morning meetings and over several cups of coffee, our leader, Ray Martinez (former mayor of Ft. Collins, Colo.), spoke about the concept of a "Godcidence; Ray explained it this way:

There is a significant difference between a coincidence and a "Godcidence." In the secular world, coincidences are an unexplained event, or as some people refer to it, as luck, chance, an accident or a fluke.

For believers, the twist of fate in God's eyes is intentional. God intended this phenomena of various events that came together simultaneously to have a changing effect on your life. This Godcidence event becomes my responsibility to respond to it by seeking God's insight and looking deep from within myself as to why God intervened at this point and time in my life .In many cases, a Godcidence is a confirmation of his divine intervention and for direction. God loves to intervene when humanoids are incapable of accomplishing such a mission.

God speaks about wanting us to test Him in Malachi 3:10: "'Bring the whole tithe into the storehouse, that there may be food in my house. Test me in this,' says the Lord Almighty, 'and see if I will not throw open the floodgates of heaven and pour out so much blessing that you will not have room enough for it.'"

No one else can do it like Him and he wants to prove Himself or validate His existence. In the Amplified Bible it reads, "Prove me." He loves it!

The Christian life is not some set of random events that simply happen. Rather, the Christian life is a carefully orchestrated plan where things happen for a reason. This has helped me to sort out the accident. It took me from being a victim to being an ambassador. It helps my feeble, rational mind accept things that, on the surface, appear to be irrational or illogical.

It grows my faith.

Lesson three: My wife has become what I've lost.

Proverbs 29:18 *"Where [there is] no vision, the people perish."*

My wife is a visionary leader.

Earlier in my career, I actually taught a class on visionary leadership. I called it "Context Leadership." Through the post-911 economic meltdown, being a manager required me to lay off many people. And the fun of a fulfilling visionary leader decayed into the chore of processing "executions" of employees. The joy of work became a routine process of traveling around the country and informing people that they were no longer needed. In fact, on one trip to the west coast, the employees knew why I was there. When they came into the conference room alone, they knew it was their time. They knew why I was visiting.

But one guy started off by saying to me, "Jim, you looked stressed. Would you like to start off our meeting with a word of prayer?" This brilliant Christian man started off our meeting with the most precious prayer that left us both in tears. And this man not only received his severance package, he also landed a better job, making more money and now gives God the glory. A Godcidence? I know so.

So on and on went the process of laying-off people. For almost three years that was my full-time job. It got to be quite easy and very process-oriented. I even created a nifty flow chart on how to fire a person. I was desensitized to the fact that I was significantly changing the lives of *people*, and became hardened to this fact. That is, until it was my time to visit my boss.

It was no shock that laying off more than one hundred people soon eroded the need for my position. On a phone call from my manager, I was summarily given my "career life expectancy" and termination date. The agony intensified as they took me on and off the list of people to be fired. I grieved the loss of my job, its security and paycheck.

Until finally one day my substitute manager called me and asked if I wanted his old job. He needed someone to substitute for him since our manager was now gone. So I agreed to step down from management and be an individual contributor.

It was during those last few years of management and then finally being demoted that my visionary leadership blood was replaced by simple survivor instincts. As I saw it, I fell a few notches on Maslow's hierarchy of needs.

Meanwhile, the converse was happening with my wife. While I was off firing people, she was growing a small eBay bookstore and learning more about Africa and the severe lack of the church's help there. My daughter traveled to Uganda to write a newspaper article about the refugees. In Aimee's words, "I wrote about Boulder's student-run Educate! nonprofit (www.educateafrica.org), which provides scholarships and leadership training to refugees and youth across Uganda. I traveled to the camp to capture the story; but as all good stories have their own uncontrollable irony, I was the one who became captured."

Aimee's article captured my wife, too. By selling books online, she raised enough money not only to assist Educate!, but to also kick off the malaria-prevention efforts. To date, more than 5,000 mosquito nets have been distributed and an orphanage and health clinic planned. Kyangwali now has at least one net per hut.

My wife is a visionary leader. After my accident, she could have given up. But she realized that it was critical for her to make this trip. So she and my daughter packed up and did it. As a result, many lives were saved.

I am extremely proud of my wife and her visionary leadership to start Think Humanity. She had a vision from her own daughter. She had a dream from her own daughter, and dreams are coming true.

In May of 2008 I was healthy enough to make the trip with Aimee and Beth to participate in "MaNdate Two," where we personally had the privilege to distribute more than 4,000 additional malaria nets, worked on the orphanage and laid out more project plans with our African administrators. I even conducted a new and improved version of my "Context Leadership" class to more than African 50 leaders! Little did I know that my personal studies of leadership would materialize in such an amazing way!

The trip was a tough one, long and a bit challenging. But our Think Humanity Admins were at the Entebbe Airport upon our arrival and that was the last time that I had to carry my 60 pound backpack. I was taken very good care of by all and they even gave me a special name, called Mzee, which is Swahili and it stands for "old and wise."

We stayed at St. Patrick's Compound right in the community of Kyangwali. An alter-boy named Joseph helped me to create a walking stick and I met many wonderful people that touched my heart with their love. I discovered that while this community was poor materialistically, they were Kings and Queens with respect to their relationship with God. They sang from their hearts, they loved with their spirit. They taught me much about God.

I am now starting to rebirth my own "Visionary Leadership" the more that I help with Think Humanity. My view of corporate work has changed; it is now a means toward the end — and not the converse. This ties into Chapter 3, in that my wife has become the type of leader that I aspire to. She has discovered the rather obvious fact that God commanded us to help the poor.

While I used to think of leadership in hierarchical corporate context, it now has expanded significantly and, more importantly, in the context that many of our great leaders are people that follow. They know when to lead, they know when to follow. They have developed the wisdom to know when to do either. Leadership is not simply having a huge corporate title sitting behind a massive oak desk overlooking some amazing vista. It is, rather, a humble experience of listening, attending and helping to play your part in the act of a positive change. I've learned that many of our great leaders are the 'feet on the ground,' the people that do the work.

In fact, positional power does not necessarily even imply that one is a leader. We can all think of cases where the 'big boss' is not respected, but we have to follow her/him, else pay the consequences. In a true leadership model, one follows from the heart, not the head.

So in all of my corporate studies on the topic of leadership, little did I realize that my wife was, in fact and unknowing even to herself, honing down her leadership skills with the work that she initiated to help people in Uganda. She screamed by me on the leadership metric and now I follow her.

Lesson four: The definition of friendship

"A man of many companions may come to ruin,
but there is a friend who sticks closer than a brother."
(Proverbs 18:24)

While a lesson about friendship might sound a bit trite, it ties back to the story of Job. During Job's suffering and trials, he had three so-called friends visit him. It says in the Book of Job that the first week, those friends just "looked at him and said nothing." Can you imagine how Job must have felt?

Then after a week of torturous silence, those three friends started to go into intellectual debate with him about his situation. These three friends were self-righteous and only served to create more stress in Job's already abysmal condition. They offered no hope for him and challenged him to "deny God and simply die." But Job did not. He persevered and his faith was bolstered. God blessed him in the end with a full recovery, physically, financially and spiritually.

In a similar disaster context more than 4,000 years later, I discovered that my true friends who really loved me simply came and spent time with me. There were many. Never once did I hear anything negative from my church buddies, my family or even acquaintances that I hadn't seen in years.

My daughter and I talked about the definition of the word "friend," and settled on a simple one: "To be there."

"Being there" doesn't mean sitting in a chair and mindlessly occupying physical space. It does mean simply holding a hand, listening and being mentally engaged. It is being present and invested, but not necessarily *doing* anything. Praying is an effective way of being there.

I remember one night in the rehab hospital, and it was very lonely. I was alone and didn't feel like reading or watching more reruns on TV. I called my son and asked if he would spend the night next to me. In less than an hour he was there, toothbrush in hand and carrying a sack of hamburgers. There were countless times when I just wanted someone to "be there" with me. I didn't want them to feel obligated to speak. Just knowing that they were there meant they loved me, which was exactly what I needed.

Another example of friendship was my best camping buddy, Tom. This guy is a high-ranked executive for a large organization and travels more than 50 percent of his time. He's constantly on the go, managing a huge organization. Tom somehow managed to visit me almost daily while I was in the hospital, and when I came home he was over every chance he could get. I have no idea how he did this, but he made being there a priority when it counted most. His wife did the same. He didn't come and offer counsel; he encouraged me, he listened to me, he was concerned and I knew this.

This ties directly into the next thing I learned.

Lesson five: The importance of the family

"Therefore, as we have opportunity, let us do good to all people, especially to those who belong to the family of believers." (Galatians 6:10)

At first, when thinking about the importance of family, my thoughts were on my direct family: my son, daughter, wife and my children in-laws. And we do have a very close-knit family.

As I've said, we have our share of problems, but we stick together. And we have some really funky traditions; one of these traditions on Christmas morning. We play a reggae Christmas CD, starting with Eek-A-Mouse's "I Wish You a Merry Christmas." And a large part of our gift exchange involves our own traditionally re-gifted gag gifts. Some of these gifts have been in the family for years and have a special and ridiculous significance, like the soap on a rope. Upon opening the soap on a rope gift, the recipient is to immediately run outside and toss it into the back yard. The roots of this tradition are now a mystery, and I'm quite confident that our neighbors (we've been living in the same house for more than 20 years) must view this as strange. Yet in during the spring thaw when I find the soap on a rope in the backyard, it always brings a smile to my face. A seemingly simple tradition, yet it is with huge meaning.

This is just one example of the fun and craziness that we share. And (somehow) it's rooted is respect and love. Lindsey, my daughter-in-law, is a graphics designer, and once she designed a poster about "The Family," modeled after the movie poster for "The Godfather." The poster represented how our family sticks together, supports each other and is quite an honor to be a part of. And once you're in, you cannot get out!

Most importantly was the message "We stick together." If someone gets bad service at a restaurant, The Family gets involved and makes it right (whatever that means). If someone's car breaks down, The Family is there. On hot summer weekend afternoons, we'll mob-wash each other's cars. We camp together. We golf together. We worship together. We laugh together and we cry together. All of these things by themselves are small acts of kindness and love, but when taken together as an aggregate picture, it's a God-given bond that is solid.

The Family has its own reputation for standing close together and supporting each other when needed. Clearly, The Family played a critical and key role during the accident, again taking on the accident as a unified problem, not just mine. We all took part of the accident, did what we could, solved one tiny piece of the puzzle at a time and helped each other. We pride ourselves in this bond and The Family has grown, adding new members along the way. And the interesting thing about The Family is that it is always growing, adopting more people along life's way. We've actually had people request if they could join The Family. Of course they could. This brings me to the next point.

The importance of the family of believers as mentioned in the Bible verse above is the broader and encompassing view of what I learned during the accident and rehab. I was constantly amazed and thankful for the dear friends that now I call my Family. We now even have the extended family in Africa and spans several other families. This Family concept is built on trust, love and support, no matter what. It crosses ethnic and geographical borders, now spanning America, Europe and Africa. By the way, we are taking membership applications for people in the Asian-Pacific Region, South America and Antarctica!

Not trying to sound haughty; all that I'm talking about here is Christ's love bonding people together in the most simplistic and yet elegant manner. As you are reading this now, you have your particular family that probably does the same. It probably has some traditional things and events that are unique. Don't take this for granted. Keep those traditional activities active. Foster expanding your family, and cherish what God has given to you!

The importance of the nuclear family is obvious and cannot be undersold. Had it not been for my wife, son, daughter, in-laws, mother and father, mother and father-in-laws and other relatives, I truly don't believe that I would have made it through the accident. The overall loving support that they poured out by the gallons gave me an inner sense of a will to live. Had I been totally alone, what reason would I have had to keep on keeping on?

During the week following the accident, my son and I were scheduled to make a 30-hour road trip to the far northern reaches of Saskatchewan for our annual Northern Pike fishing adventure. That didn't happen, but I got a full refund, and we will resume this very fine tradition in the future. My son and I started this tradition when he was 9 years old. He is now 26. I'm looking forward to the day when we take his son to Canada and keep this tradition alive.

The importance of the extended family, which includes Christian brothers and sisters, friends, co-workers, pastors, prayer warriors and others also injected into my soul more love than I could imagine. During my first few days in ICU, my daughter placed a journal book in my room where people could sign in, make comments, prayers and share miscellaneous feelings.

Here is some of what I found in my journal when I could finally read it, along with some of my comments about some of the journal entries. This is my web of support.

"Only in a world where faith is difficult can faith truly exist."
- Text sent to Beth from C.

"Well, it would have killed a mortal man."
— From R.V.

"He gives strength to the weary and increases the power of the weak."
— Isaiah 40:29

"God is our refuge and strength, an ever present help in trouble."
— Psalm 46:1, Aimee's favorite passage

"If you believe, you will receive, whatever you ask for in prayer."
— Matthew 21:22

"Jim, we don't know what a day will bring, do we? God doesn't keep us from the storms, but he's with us in the midst of it — giving power, strength and courage. You're such a servant of Him, He will never leave you. I'm praying your recovery is quick and miraculous. You are a blessed man to have the family you have, who are praying, crying and loving you through this. I see Jesus in them. Let The Master heal you!" — From pastor J.S.

"Hey special Frog, We are praying for you in your healing. You have had so many people stop in to see you. You have touched many, many lives. I hope you know how loved you are! God has some special plans for you. May your healing be so rapid and smooth that it astounds the doctors. We are all so blessed that you are still with us. We look forward to many, many, many 'moons' being with you!!! I love you!" – From P.B.

"Jim, Our thoughts and prayers are with you. We love you and so much appreciate the witness and testimony you are. We are blessed by you and your love for our Lord. Keep the course. Jer 29:11. God has great plans for you. He is bigger than our circumstances." — From D and K

"Ken and I are praying for your rapid recovery! God will see you thru this time!! As the song says, 'I don't know about tomorrow, but I know who holds my hands.'" — From Dave

"Jim, there's a ton of people praying for you, even in China. D.A. wants to talk to you from China. Hopefully you two can connect soon. Remember, a hit like you took would have killed a mortal man. Must mean you are a tough guy. You'll have a story to tell when this is all over. You're family's <u>faith</u> is really impressing me. They are super strong! I've never seen such a close-knit family. Get better soon." –From R.V.

(My comment)
I'm not sure about my "immortality," but the comment was made twice by the same person on two separate occasions, and it challenged me to think of the balance of my mortal life and what I am going to do with it. I realize that I am mortal physically, but I

also know that I am playing on an immortal team with God as my coach.

"Jim, best wishes for a speedy recovery! You're a good man. Make it your mission to not see me next weekend, 'cause that would mean you've been here way too long!"— From a nurse

"Our most important job now is to protect him from sound."— From Nathan

(My Comment)
Nathan was always looking to solve the next problem and continually looking out for me.

"I feel like a brand new man."— Me after my "bed bath"

"Something good will come out of this. Just believe."— From Damian

"Frog always tells me 'I love you' when saying goodbye, every time when we hang out. I hate this to happen to you frog, but I just want to do everything I can to help you and the family to show I love you too!"—From Aaron,

"I've been praying my heart out. For every tear that falls, a prayer is said for you and frog, my sweet frog, and you." — From D.C., in a text message to Aimee

"W.S. called and is very concerned and sends his love and prayers."— From a voice mail

"From Katie: Maggie has enjoyed the chocolate donuts and dancing with Nate. Frog, I think you're awesome, and we are all praying for you. Sonic milkshakes are on me next time!"

"Frog, I'm truly amazed by your heart and strength. At first I questioned, "Why? Why this would all happen to a great man of

God?" But then I realized what I was saying and saw Satan was trying to take over my thoughts, too. He has interrupted in a huge way, but I hope we can all continue to see God's master plan through it all, too. I'll leave you with one quote that I fell in love with and I hope it gives you strength at those points when God may be a far reach: 'Only in a world where faith is difficult can faith truly exist.' It's not always going to be easy but know you have an incredibly strong family, awesome friends and an amazing God to turn to. Much love XOXOXO."— From C.C.

"You were awake and asked me how I am doing. It meant a lot when you prayed that I would have peace. It was hard to witness your best friend and father go through the worst thing you have ever seen. I feel the peace that you prayed for."— From Nathan, 11:35 p.m. one night.

"I was totally blessed by a smile from someone who has been through so much. James opened his eyes and smiled!!! His family smiled!!! For me, an awesome smile from God penetrated the entire room. He is at work. I have been blessed by a loving son, wife, daughter and many others over the past few days. Truly, God is in this place. His love, joy and healing are in place. God bless them all in the days to come and continue to let HIS love shine in what we do. God's Love!"— From Pastor Michael, chaplain,

From our extended African family and Think Humanity administrators: Psalms 34:19, 46:1-3, 32:7, 2 Cor. 1:7, Nahum 1:7. Beth read these verses to me.

From voice mails at home: Multiple messages from Dave, Crystal, Pam, Tiffers, my mom, my sis, Lynn, Cindy, Gene, John H., John S., and many more offering help and prayers.

"Jim, I want you to know how sorry I am this happened to you. But I know you are in God's hands and we are, will be, praying for you. You will be made strong again. I love you, brother." –From Wally.

"We started with a work relationship, but we have become friends as brothers in Christ. It has been a great joy and encouragement to me to see your growth and to be challenged by your faith and dedication. I know God has kept you at (work) for a purpose — and part of that purpose has been my growth. I'm looking forward to fellowship and encouragement soon — and for eternity." — From Mike

"I dedicated my fishing trip today to you, but the good Lord wanted me to come to see you instead so he sent thunder and lightning and chased me off the river (North Fork of the Poudre). So I came to see you — but you were sleeping. We love you." — Pam and Joe,

"Frog, right now you're lying here, caught halfway between your dreams and another episode of 'Survivorman.' While you chuckle at the Survivorman's ability to stay alive another day in the cold North Arctic plains of Canada, you have been involuntarily casted to the role of Survivorman for everyone else around you to watch and admire. All the skills and knowledge you have acquired up until now are being requested and first and foremost your ability to completely and wholeheartedly trust God to lead you. You are currently fighting a fight that only you can understand, but with God's love and everlasting support you will come out victorious. Love you dearly." — From Damian,

"Several weeks ago you told me you were praying for a miracle. A miracle like the one that brought Lindsey and me back from Texas. You prayed for a miracle at that time, and you were put in the middle of it. This time, more seems like it is on the line and you told me you are scared to be part of it. You even said something big would happen and you didn't know if you could face sacrificing your life for it. How did you know? How did you decide that you would go to the brink of death? You must have looked Satan in the eye and said, 'I fear no evil, fear is feeling that evil put in you.' Did you stand up to fear and say, 'Use my life; I am not afraid?' I can only assume that you knew, and the fact that you accepted this as the miracle is nothing short of a miracle in itself. I have the necklace right now, something that we have passed back and forth since I was only 7 or so. I gave it back to you when our family found Christ just a couple of years ago. It was handed to me in the emergency room, and I knew you were telling me something: 'Be strong, Nate. I need you to support the family right now.' I didn't think I would ever be able to give you back this responsibility that can at times feel like a burden. You kept me prepared, kept me focused like a trained fighter and did not let me wander because you were preparing me. You are a general that has led your family to battles against evil and right now is your most glorious moment. Be proud because the riches you have stored up in Heaven are uncountable and your love will tear through the ugly heart of this world until our God returns. You amaze me. — Son

PS: The beauty in this is incredible; your light is casting out across the world."

"Frog, You mean the world to my family and me! You and your loved ones have been in my thoughts and prayers. I cannot tell you how thankful I am to still have you in my life! You are an amazing Christian role model and extremely loving family man! I always enjoy talking to you and listening to your stories! God is definitely watching over you! I will continue to pray for a fast recovery."— From Tiffers,

"Frog: Not bad for an old man who got run over. We are so glad you are doing so well! You are so loved and we are all praying for a quick recovery. I'll never forget singing songs down in Mississippi tearing out the walls! We love you!"— From Bill, referring to a recent mission trip we experienced together to help with the rebuilding of the Gulf Coast after Hurricane Katrina.

"Dear Frog, Get better soon! You are an amazing dad, based on your family. You have a wonderful family and a wonderful spirit. You are recovering so well — please keep at it!"— From Claire,

"Jim, Nate was doing wheelies in your wheelchair!"— From Beth

"You said the life of a Christian is very purposeful. No coincidences. If you're gonna ask for a miracle, you'd better be ready to be pulled into it. I came to a realization if I am going to be in a miracle, I don't have to be ridiculously fearful of God jacking me around. If this has made people think a little deeper about Christ, then it's worth it." — From me, although I don't recall saying it.

When I returned home and had some time to collect my thoughts and organize my life, spending time reading and re-reading these comments that people wrote during some of my weakest hours. These comments amazed me, and it almost felt as if I had died and was now reading my funeral registry of those who attended my wake. I cried with the love that was there, yet I had been taking for granted for many, many years.

The lesson: *Appreciate and love your immediate and extended family.*

Even as families have breaks in relationships, experience divorces, adopt children and have blended families that are seemingly awkward, this immediate family is a source of strength and a gift from God. In the broadest contextual definition of the word "family," enjoy it, cherish it and love one another on a daily basis. Don't be afraid to overuse the words, "I love you," even in short text messages, e-mails or when you're saying goodbye for the evening. Those three words set the amazing stage for a life play that is magnificent, even if some of the scenes are not fun.

Bonded together in love for eternity.

Lesson six: The importance of the local church

"After all, no one ever hated his own body, but he feeds and cares for it, just as Christ does the church." (Ephesians 5:29)

As I've pointed out in my history, our family only recently returned to "the church." We are now members of our local church and love it. Before the accident, I felt independent, priding myself on the fact that "I didn't need too many friends," and clearly had no need for the association with fellow Christians in the form of church. For almost 20 years, we only frequented church on Easter and Christmas, and that was enough.

Now things are different. God is in the business of changing lives, and He's turned mine around, demonstrating His amazing patience and unending love that I cannot begin to comprehend. Being associated with fellow believers in Jesus helps me tremendously. It helps me to lean on them in fellowship and worship and share each other's pains and trials. We have a kindred of hearts, knitted closely together through Jesus. After coming back to God, joining our church and rededicating my life to Christ, I figured I would not have any more problems. I figured that giving up drinking could be topped by nothing more. Little did I know that the Evil One was lurking on the sidelines, hating everything that I was now about.

To say that my church played a huge role in the *active demonstration of Christ's Love* is a huge understatement. Prior to the accident, our church had just finished up a series called "The Summer of Love," where sermons focused on the "active love" that we need to show in our families, friends and the local church. I can honestly say that had it not been for my local church members offering help – physically, spiritually and emotionally – we all would have collapsed. It was too much to carry alone. I am thankful to God that my brothers and sisters in Christ actively demonstrated what it means to have Christ's Love in the heart.

For starters, a crew (led by my son) re-outfitted my house to make it wheelchair accessible. They brought in a real hospital bed (the details which Lindsey secured), built ramps and retrofitted the entire downstairs so that I could get around. They took care of my lawn, sprinkler system, garage, trash and it seemed anything I needed was only a phone call away.

Each one of my three church pastors frequently came to visit, stayed in touch, e-mailed me and led the church praying for me. They did this while I was in the hospital and, maybe more importantly, during the long recovery. It was not a parachute charity act. They were committed to stand by me for the long haul. Prayers make a huge difference, and to have more than 1,000 people praying for you is an amazing blessing. And it's only by those prayers that I am able to write these words right now. Praise God for the local church.

I remember when I could finally physically return to worship in our church. I was swarmed by my Christian brothers and sisters. While still in a wheelchair, the music and message sounded especially sweet.

1 Thes 5:16-18 says, *"Be joyful always; pray continually; give thanks in all circumstances, for this is God's will for you in Christ Jesus."*

My church is where the workweek is overwhelmed by the presence of God, where it's just a small sampling taste of what heaven must be like. God's love was dramatically demonstrated by my church.

Lesson seven: People with handicaps need our special consideration and love

"The King will reply, 'I tell you the truth, whatever you did for one of the least of these brothers of mine, you did for me.'" (Matthew 25:40)

My dad was in World War II and is an extremely decorated soldier, holding two Purple Hearts, a Bronze Star and many other noteworthy medals for his service for our country. He was in the Normandy Invasion and almost died on Omaha Beach, on the north coast of France. He is also a brilliant Christian man. His legs were severely damaged during the war, leaving him 80 percent handicapped. He was hit multiple times by large caliber bullets and hand grenades. I grew up living with a handicapped father. He still managed to play softball and take me fishing. He camouflaged his physical limitations to the point that I did not really appreciate his condition — until I found myself with my own limitations after the accident.

I learned an important, yet too obvious, fact: people with handicaps need our special consideration and love. Little things are huge deals to a person with a disability. Making a cup of coffee, even just having to reach for a cup in a cupboard, can be an ordeal if things are not engineered for a wheelchair person.

After returning home from the hospital, I realized how much I took the little things for granted. Little things became huge obstacles. Most homes are not designed for people with handicaps. Getting in and out of a car is a huge deal. Going out for dinner and having people look at you in a weird way.

For a while, my showers were out on our back patio (wearing boxers for the sake of the neighbors!), where we draped the kitchen sink's spray hose through a window. Our ground floor had no shower, and I could not get up the two flights of stairs to the other bathrooms. Fortunately, it was late summer, so the temperature afforded this arrangement. This process took the help of my wife and usually consumed the better part of an hour, putting my legs in plastic bags to keep the equipment dry. I remember the first time I managed to crawl backwards to our upstairs master bathroom and sat on the floor of our shower and took my first real shower indoors, without a hose. What a seemingly simple, but radically important event!

During my home rehab, I watched the show "Survivorman" on the Discovery Channel. Les Stroud is an amazing guy, and his outdoor survivor tips actually applied directly to me in the confines of my rehab environment, making effective use of the limited resources at one's disposal. It utilized the same principles: Setting daily goals, using resources that are available and figuring out contingency plans for survival. It all made too much sense, and I think I watched the entire series at least five times.

Whatever the particular disability is, people with handicaps need people without handicaps to be more sensitive and helpful. Those handicapped parking places really make a huge difference. Perhaps this is obvious, but the appreciation that I learned having gone through the accident really drove home my need to have compassion and love for people with any handicap. By enduring it first-hand, it really drives home the gravity of the fact. Because of the accident, I will always have a deeper compassion and love for people with any handicap

Chapter 7

When (not if) You're Hit from Behind

Life can change in a second. We all will be or have been hit from behind.

"Do not boast about tomorrow, for you do not know what a day may bring forth."(Proverbs27:1)

One moment things were absolutely perfect, riding alongside my son on a bright and sunny summer afternoon in Colorado.
The very next second, life changed dramatically. I didn't know what hit me, had no control and that split second set into motion events that my family and I will live with forever.

I praise God that my spiritual condition was not in a mess; else I truly do not believe that I would have made it through the Black Room. Make no mistake, this is not about *me* and how great of a Christian I am. My historical track record proves this not to be the case, and I am ashamed of that. This is not a piety lecture. It is, however, a challenge to "center" your own Christian life.

I believe that God has His **Perfect Will** for us as Christians. This Perfect Will is the original design of our lives as God would have it. In my case, however, I blew achieving His Perfect Will, because of the choices I made that took me off His perfect path.

But the good news is that God also has His **Circumstantial Will**, which allows us to take our life circumstances (if they are blemished, which they are in everyone's case) and turn them into a purposeful life. Many Bible teachers use different terms to describe God's Will, but the point is that even a jacked-up person can find meaning through trusting in Christ. No matter how bad the circumstances, Christ can make the difference.

I am thankful to God for His patience with me. Also, since we don't know when something is going to hit us from behind, our lives need to be centered on Christ. Being hit from behind can take on many forms, ranging from health problems to relationship issues, but at some point in time, it will happen to all of us. Having Christ with you to endure it makes all the difference! My lead pastor said it best: "It doesn't matter where you've been, but it does matter where you are at now." As Christians, we are either *growing in* The Lord or *growing from* The Lord. There is no middle ground where we're just statically maintaining the status quo.

As Christians, we are to be slaves to righteousness. In Romans chapter 6 we read, *"What then? Shall we sin because we are not under law but under grace? By no means! Don't you know that when you offer yourselves to someone to obey him as slaves, you are slaves to the one whom you obey — whether you are slaves to sin, which leads to death, or to obedience, which leads to righteousness? But thanks be to God that, though you used to be slaves to sin, you wholeheartedly obeyed the form of teaching to which you were entrusted. You have been set free from sin and have become slaves to righteousness."*

This is one of my favorite passages in the Bible, and it challenges us to grow up as Christians and die to our old selves on a daily basis. Just hours before I left for my son's house I wrote this in my journal:

Father God, Abba,
Thank You Lord for saving my soul.
Thank You for allowing me to see You someday.
Thank You for another day of life
A fine job
Bible study this morning
A fine and healthy family
A loving and caring wife with a vision to change Africa
Two perfect children and in-law kids
True and perfect parents
More resources than I need
Health, joy and contentment
Blessing me with some gifts

For being so patient with me
The rains last night
The freshness of this new day and your promise to help me
Lord Jesus Christ, I may not always display it with works, but I love you dearly.
Higher than the highest mountains,
Deeper than the deepest sea,
Love,
Jim (Frog)

The key lesson in this accident is just because we get our lives fixed on God doesn't mean that we won't have problems. It's how we handle those problems that makes the difference between having joy in bad situations, else frustration. I'm learning this now. I have *seen the resolve* in my wife and daughter's eyes as they talked about leaving me in the hospital and continuing their trip to Uganda. I have *felt my daughter holding my hand throughout the night,* sleeping in a chair next to my bed. I have *seen the amazing love of my son and his wife* as they spent countless hours simply being in the hospital room with me, keeping me company and taking care of my house. I have *witnessed some of our otherwise distant family members, becoming much closer.*

I now Praise God for this situation! Even though it was (and always will be) wrought with much pain, torture, loss and even an upcoming third surgery on my right leg. The probability of additional surgeries is also high. But I clearly learned and witnessed the love of Christ in my family and church brothers and sisters. I also learned that *each day that God gives to us is a gift.* He grants life to all of us. I learned that your life can change in one second, when an innocent person simply takes his mind off of driving for just a second. And most importantly, the accident makes me know in my heart that God is in control of all things.

Romans 5:1-11 sums it up perfectly: "Therefore, since we have been justified through faith, we have peace with God through our Lord Jesus Christ, through whom we have gained access by faith into this grace in which we now stand. And we boast in the hope of the glory of God. Not only so, but we also glory in our sufferings, because we know that suffering produces perseverance; perseverance, character; and character, hope. And hope does not put us to shame, because God's love has been poured out into our hearts through the Holy Spirit, who has been given to us. You see, at just the right time, when we were still powerless, Christ died for the ungodly. Very rarely will anyone die for a righteous person, though for a good person someone might possibly dare to die. But God demonstrates his own love for us in this: While we were still sinners, Christ died for us. Since we have now been justified by his blood, how much more shall we be saved from God's wrath through him! For if, while we were God's enemies, we were reconciled to him through the death of his Son, how much more, having been reconciled, shall we be saved through his life! Not only is this so, but we also boast in God through our Lord Jesus Christ, through whom we have now received reconciliation."

The Christian life is not an easy one. If you are trying to live for God, then most certainly it will anger the Evil One and this negative spiritual force will be on the attack daily. The Christian life will be a challenging one, and we must grow up in Christ in order to handle these challenges in a way that glorifies God, especially when we're hit from behind.

Staying in God's will is akin to driving in your lane and putting on the full armor of God so we can withstand the problems that come up. How we handle these problems will either make us grow closer to God, or we'll drift from Him.

Implicit here is the sense of having joy as a Christian, knowing that God is in control of everything. We tend to live either in the past (regret or pride) or the future (anticipation and greed), and we sometimes miss the present moment. It's almost as if we need to s-t-r-e-t-c-h out the present, and enjoy the particular moment where we are at, even amid troubles. This brings true joy, relaxing in the arms of God, allowing Him to take the "handlebars of life" and guide us.

This story is about a car-bike accident. But metaphorically, we all get hit from behind, whether it be the loss of a job, the death of a loved one, a disease, a divorce, a friend who hurts you, a marriage conflict, a missed promotional opportunity, a sickness or even having a bad hair day. And if you haven't *yet* been hit from behind, it's only a matter of time. That is not to say, "Hey, get ready for some really bad times, and expect the worst!" It is to say, however, that our mortal lives are not always going to be smooth sailing, and how we handle the rough rogue waves makes all of the difference. How do you handle being hit from behind?

My prayer and hope is that if you are not a Christian, then you'll consider God, who He is and what you are doing about it. Maybe it will take a hard hit to jolt you into this consideration. Maybe it will take another Sept. 11 disaster. Maybe it will simply take quiet time, your heart and listening to how God is speaking. He may be speaking to you right now.

Frankly, I don't know how to survive without God. And to roll a bit of logic into this equation, if I'm wrong on this "God thing," and we all end up in heaven some day, then no big deal. I didn't miss out on anything. But if it is true about Christ being the only way to heaven — the *only* way — then death will have an ugly and eternal sting for the unbeliever. And I know, through faith, that He is the only way. As Hebrews 11:1 says, "Now faith is being sure of what we hope for and certain of what we do not see."

My prayer for the Christian is that you thank God for your salvation. Do it right now; He's listening to your thoughts as you read this. And if you've given your heart to Christ, then ponder the question: "Have I given my life to Him?" Again, I'm still working on this one and have "miles to go before I sleep, miles to go. ..."

And whether it's on a bike ride, a horse ride, working in a bakery, going to work one day at the World Trade Center, traveling on a remote highway at night, trusting your spouse to be faithful, trying to make a decent living or just hanging out with a friend drinking coffee, we all WILL be – it is not a question of probability- hit from behind. And what we do with that hit will make all of the difference.

Because we do not know when or how we will be hit from behind, it challenges us to live each day as if it were our last. It might be.

Psalm 60:16: *"I will sing of your love; for you are my fortress, my refuge in times of trouble."*

Thank you for listening to this story.
Jim Heckel

Printed in the United States
136508LV00011B/265/P

9 781607 910343